THE INSIDER'S EDGE

MAXIMIZING INVESTMENT PROFITS THROUGH MANAGED FUTURES ACCOUNTS

BERTRAM SCHUSTER
HOWARD ABELL

Probus Publishing Company
Chicago, Illinois

Library of Congress Cataloging in Publication Data

Schuster, Bertram.
  The insider's edge.

  Includes index.
  1. Commodity exchanges--United States.
2. Investments--United States--Management.
I. Abell, Howard. II. Title.
HG6046.S38 1985   332.64'4'0973   85-6592
ISBN 0-917253-12-4

Library of Congress Catalog Card No. 85-6592

Printed in the United States of America

1 2 3 4 5 6 7 8 9 0

Joint Dedication

First mention must go to our clients, trading advisors, and publisher, for without them this book would not exist.

Bertram Schuster's Dedication

To George Segal, who gave me my start; Arthur Marcus, who keeps me going; Debbie Polin, who has assisted me from the very beginning; Frank Pusateri, a most knowledgeable and professional consultant; Wallace Roberts, who counseled me; Sy Nagorski, an accountant who really goes beyond the numbers; Phil Grossfield, a great person; and, of course, Teena Schuster, who in her own wonderful way provided inspiration, encouragement, and guidance.

An author's indulgence to my children: Jennifer, Ravelle, Bart, and Ian.

Howard Abell's Dedication

To George Segal, a valued friend and business partner for many years; Debbie Polin, whose able assistance began even before this book was begun; Frank Pusateri, who helped to introduce me to the managed account industry; and especially to my wife Roslyn for the support and intellectual input required to complete this project.

An author's indulgence to my son, Alexander.

Preface

This book is designed to help the investor who, being buffeted by an erratic economy and volatile markets, frequently experiences disappointing investment results. It shares with the investor lessons learned over years of active participation in a variety of investment markets. Through thousands of hours of their own time and a significant amount of their own capital, the authors have developed a highly disciplined investment approach that can immediately benefit *all* investors, whether or not they have previously been successful.

The reader is unlikely to hear the information presented in *The Insider's Edge* from a stock or commodity broker. The disciplined approach to managed commodity futures investing outlined here requires substantial, specialized expertise. Furthermore, most brokers do not like to relinquish "control" of your money, even to a full-time, successful professional. In addition, the total amount normally paid in commissions in managed account programs such as the one described in this book is significantly lower than that required by other, alternative investment programs.

As registered stock and commodity brokers familiar with a wide range of investment vehicles, we recommend that you seriously consider investing a portion of your assets in a program similar to the one we describe in the following pages. If you are now investing, or have previously invested, in stocks, bonds, or money market funds, this book is for you.

We have attempted to keep this book free of jargon and technical terminology, so that, regardless of your familiarity with commodities, it will be both comprehensible and practical. We have also attempted to make each chapter, in and of itself, a source of readily accessible information, so that the reader can benefit from any given chapter at any time. Our chart (Chapter 4) on winners and losers in stock and commodity investing can save you far more than the cost of the book.

The approach to futures investing advocated in these pages is not a get-rich-quick scheme. It is a conservative, *disciplined*, diversified, and professionally managed approach. It offers risk control, regulatory protection, favorable tax treatment, competitive rates of return, performance-related compensation provisions, cost controls, and an array of other benefits that can make *all* your investments work better for you.

Onward to successful investing!

Bertram Schuster
Howard Abell

Contents

Chapter
1

What's Missing in Your Investments?

Why your portfolio, as presently structured, cannot perform well in times of deflation, recession, inflation, or high interest rates.

Why you should consider broader diversification of your investments.

While the universe of investment vehicles available to the individual investor has expanded significantly in recent years, today's typical investor steers investments onto a rather narrow and traditional track. Despite the increasing economic uncertainty of the past two decades—accompanied by unprecedented high interest and inflation rates and the resulting greater volatility of the stock and bond markets—investors on the whole have stayed with a traditional portfolio mix limited to exchange-listed stocks and an assortment of bonds, government securities, money market instruments, and tax shelters.

While some investors have recently begun to look in new directions, much of the expansion of the average investor's portfolio has been in the stock market, with greater diversification influenced by the growth of modern portfolio theory and its variations. According to that theory, the risks associated with the ownership of stocks in specific companies and industries can be reduced through greater stock portfolio diversification.

However, one component of risk, *market risk,* cannot be reduced by simple stock diversification. Market risk affects all stocks to some degree. Broad market forces, such as interest rate volatility and inflation—or even the mere intimation of these—will produce widespread stock price activity, up, down, and sideways. Regardless of how many stocks from an array of different industries are contained in it, a stock portfolio is and will remain susceptible to the risks, volatility, and vagaries of the market as a whole.

Taking a cue from the portfolio managers of the larger institutional investors, some individual investors have attempted to combine a limited degree of stock diversification with an asset-shifting approach. During bear markets, for example, many investors have opted to shift a large percentage of their assets out of stocks and into money-market or similar interest-rate instruments. When, on the other hand, interest rates start to fall and stock prices begin to rise, investors generally will shift more of their assets back into the equity markets.

While the securities markets have grown increasingly reactive to swings in interest rates, widespread use of stock market diversification strategies, particularly by large institutional investors, have served to increase volatility. This added volatility has in turn resulted in a "flattening-out" of the market's performance over time. The efficiencies of the market and the sheer massiveness of institutional portfolios have begun to severely limit what the individual investor can do to achieve real diversification using stocks alone.

A more efficient and a more sophisticated level of portfolio diversification is clearly required to help increase returns and reduce risks. But before we examine the type of new diversification to adopt, let us take a brief look at some of the problems faced by the typical stock and bond investor under a variety of recent economic conditions.

Problems Faced by Investors

First, it is clear that despite higher yields, real rates of return on cash equivalent positions, such as money market funds, are affected negatively by high rates of inflation and the erosion of capital that such inflation brings—even during periods of high interest rates.

Even more striking is the impact of inflation on stocks. In Figure 1-1, the Dow Jones Industrial Average since 1950 is compared with a Dow index adjusted for inflation, using the Consumer Price Index as the measure of inflation during this period. Here we can see a marked deterioration in the index adjusted for inflation, particularly for the 16 year period from 1966 to 1982. The dotted line, representing the value of the Dow Jones Average adjusted for inflation, shows a significant loss of purchasing power in these years. During this period, holders of long-term fixed-yield notes saw their capital depreciate under the weight of inflation, and were unable to take advantage of several sharp upward turns in interest rates brought about by the relatively lower fixed yields.

Hurt by increased volatility in the securities markets and in interest rates during most of the post-war period, and by high rates of inflation, today's investor has begun to look for a means of achieving a more advanced level of portfolio diversification. Investors would like to further diversify their equity positions, thereby protecting their portfolios against interest rate swings and cyclical stock market swings. In addition, investors need investment instruments capable of providing sufficient diversification and flexibility to deal with the effects of inflation or, for that matter, deflation, recession, and high interest rates.

The dismal performance of the stock market during the long years of "stagflation" in the 1970s gave way to the rise

Figure 1–1
Stripping Inflation from Stock Prices

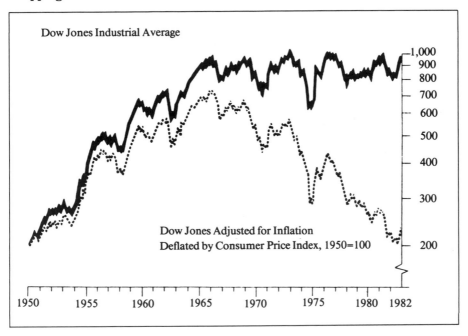

Sources: Dow Jones & Company, Bureau of Labor Statistics (consumer price data). Copyright ©1983/1984 by The New York Times Company. Reprinted by permission.

Illustrated here is the striking impact of inflation on stocks. When the Dow Jones Industrial Average since 1950 is compared with a Dow index adjusted for inflation, we can see a marked deterioration in the index for the 16-year period from 1966 to 1982.

of deflationary forces in 1980 and 1981 and again in 1984. During this most recent period interest rates have tended to drop from their previous incredible heights, and rates of inflation have moderated, but mounting federal budget deficits have been a key factor in keeping real interest rates (adjusted for inflation) relatively high. This, in turn, has helped to boost the value of the U.S. dollar, but at the expense of American exports, causing a potential choke point for economic recovery.

By way of illustration, look at Figure 1-2, "How the Trade and Budget Deficits Have Soared," which appeared in the December 19, 1984 *New York Times*. The federal budget deficit has grown from about 58 billion dollars in 1980 to an estimated 177 billion dollars in 1984. Similarly, the national trade deficit has grown from about eight billion dollars to 123 billion in the same period. This combination of soaring federal budget and foreign trade deficits could result in a return to the days of high interest rates, renewed inflation and reduced economic activity. The 1982 bull market in common stocks was a tremendous relief for many traditional equity investors and their portfolios, but that bull market has not been able to sustain itself since August, 1983, under the combined pressures of high real interest rates, budget deficits, and an uncertain future for both the domestic and world economies.

It is this uncertainty that generally pervades the current estimates and predictions of economists and investment advisors alike. Some experts conclude that we are headed for a period of renewed inflation, while others offer equally convincing arguments that as of year-end 1984 we are already well into another major recession. It is useful, therefore, to examine some of the most recent indicators.

Figure 1–2
How the Trade and Budget Deficits Have Soared
Federal Budget Deficit (Adjusted to Remove Cyclical Factors) and
the Current Account Balance; Both Quarterly Data at Annual Rates.
in Billions of Dollars)

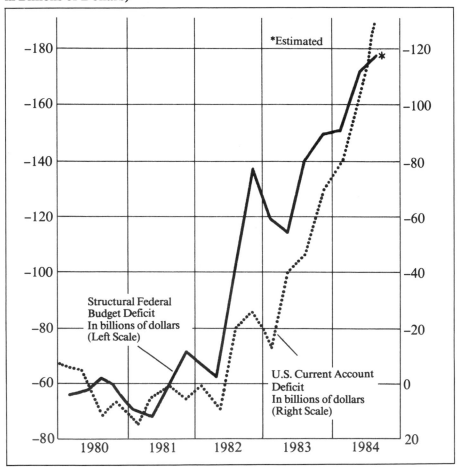

Source: Goldman, Sachs. Copyright ©1983/1984 by The New York Times Company. Reprinted by permission.

This figure shows the growth of the federal budget deficit from about 58 billion dollars in 1980 to an estimated 177 billion dollars in 1984 and the national trade deficit from about 8 billion dollars to nearly 130 billion in the same period.

An Uncertain Economy

In addition to the staggering trade and budget deficits already cited, we should note that the 18-month period from July 1983 to the end of 1984 saw the lowest level of personal savings in the United States for any 18-month period during the last 35 years. A mid-year 1984 decline in housing starts was accompanied by a similar slump in retail sales. A combination of unusually high business inventories, declining use of industrial and commercial capacity, and a 13-percent drop in new orders for capital equipment from May through December 1984, could help produce a recession that is both steep and deep, and possibly prolonged. That would mean the third recession in only five years (the first having occurred from February to August of 1980; the second, from August of 1981 to December of 1982).

Global economic contraction, falling commodity and raw materials prices, and spiraling debt service requirements have continued to wear upon the already frayed fabric of the international financial system. At least 40 developing nations are considered near default on significant portions of their foreign loans, many of these loans being held by the largest U.S. commercial and investment banks. Federal agencies reportedly list nearly 800 U.S. banks on their roster of "problem banks," a situation which is compounded by the estimated 190 billion dollars owed to domestic financial institutions by the hundreds of thousands of farmers threatened by high interest rates and low commodity and land prices.

We have rapidly become a debtor nation. In recent years, the United States was alone among major industrial nations in increasing total debt as a percentage of Gross National Product. And it is this growing consumer and government debt, in the midst of yet another economic contraction, which could bring about a renewal of inflation.

The 14-percent boost in the money supply, which helped to fuel the last recovery from July 1982 to May 1983, is still felt in the Consumer Price Index (CPI) inflation rate. Even at a relatively modest 4.3 percent (actual annual rate of inflation for 1984) inflation is still historically high by peacetime standards. It might be useful to recall that in August of 1971, then-President Richard M. Nixon invoked wage and price controls when the inflation rate was a mere 3.4 percent! If the current four percent annual inflation rate should, by some chance persist, the value of a dollar would be cut in half in 18 years. And it is certainly within the realm of possibility that the Federal Reserve will attempt to push the economy out of another recession by its traditional means: pumping up the money supply and perhaps triggering a new round of double-digit inflation.

In Table 1–1 we can see the devastating effects of various rates of inflation on an investor's $100,000 in cash. Even at a 6-percent inflation rate, $100,000 loses more than 25 percent of its value in only five years, and the situation worsens with higher inflation rates over longer periods of time. With inflation at 10 percent over 25 years, for example, $100,000 dwindles to a mere $9,230. That's a depreciation of more than 90 percent in the course of one generation.

We are currently walking too thin a tightrope over the possibility of renewed inflation, unsustained economic recovery, and the threat of deflation and recession for any but the most naive investor to believe that certainty and security have returned to the investment world. Uncertainty has again become business-as-usual.

Are we then to say that modern portfolio theory, based on the prudent allocation of assets and their ample diversification, has become obsolete? Quite the contrary. Shifting the allocation of assets in response to a variety of market conditions can be an effective although somewhat limited

Table 1–1
What Today's $100,000 Will Be Worth

Annual Rate of Inflation	Today	In 5 Years	In 15 Years	In 25 Years
6%	$100,000	$74,726	$41,727	$23,300
8	100,000	68,058	31,524	14,602
10	100,000	62,092	23,939	9,230
12	100,000	56,743	18,270	5,882
14	100,000	51,937	14,010	3,779

This table shows the devastating effects of inflation on an investor's portfolio. Inflation of 10% over 25 years reduces $100,000 to a mere $9,230.

approach. Similarly, portfolio diversification to reduce investment risk is indeed a sound investment principle.

What most investors lack is a sufficiently broad application of the positive features of modern portfolio theory to their investments. What is needed are disciplined financial instruments to provide a means of further diversifying normal equity positions, to reduce the downside risks inherent in the typical stock and bond portfolio, and to increase the average annual rate of return of a typical equity-based portfolio under a wide variety of economic and market conditions.

Where Do Investors Look for More Efficient Diversification?

Some investors have sought investment vehicles in a variety of areas, primarily as inflation hedges. Hard commodities, precious metals (such as gold), real estate, art objects, coins, and other collectibles have attracted an increasing share of investor interest during the past two decades. Real estate tax shelters are particularly attractive as devices to protect capital from the dual ravages of inflation and taxes. Yet, along with other hard commodities, real estate values themselves have fluctuated greatly reacting to a broad spectrum of economic and market conditions.

The 1980s tax laws encouraged over-investment in real estate, a situation which may have helped many investors shelter their funds but which has also caused office vacancy rates to exceed 20 percent in many cities. Many hotel and motel developments are suffering from low occupancy rates, even after cutting their rates, and sunbelt condominium foreclosures have become a frequent occurrence. Now, many economists predict that the Treasury's "tax simplification" plan, if enacted, will depress home values and restrict many real estate tax benefits for the investor.

A fundamental problem for most investors seeking adequate protection through investing in hard commodities and collectibles lies in the nature of these markets. The investor will frequently buy at retail prices and sell at wholesale prices. In addition, these markets require a level of study and involvement beyond the scope of all but the most highly specialized experts and professionals.

Even during periods of rapid appreciation in the prices of such alternative vehicles as gold coins or bullion, art objects, or other collectibles, the investor's real return will be significantly reduced by such factors as storage and insurance costs, and hidden opportunity costs including the lack of interest earned on such investments.

In short, some investors' hard commodities and collectibles can serve as an inflation hedge, but for the traditional conservative investor the disadvantages often out-weigh the advantages.

It is within this context that we can begin to consider the unique role that the market for commodity futures, when approached conservatively using a professionally managed and diversified portfolio, can play in reducing investment risk and increasing overall returns from an investor's portfolio.

Chapter
2

How Commodity Futures Can Help You Profit under Different Economic Conditions

Preserving capital and creating wealth in the present uncertain investment environment.

Comparing your portfolio mix with one ideal for today's economy.

Why futures, when added to your existing investments, can reduce overall investment risk and achieve your investment objectives.

A comparison of the effectiveness of commodity futures with other investments.

Shifting economic conditions, highly volatile markets, and an uncertain future face every investor. The ravages of inflation, recession, deflation, and high interest rates can, as we have seen in the previous chapter, create disturbing risks for the traditional portfolio. Now, let us examine how *commodity futures* can help reduce those risks, increase your investment returns, and help you meet your investment goals.

Goals of Today's Investor

Despite the changing shape of today's investment world, the primary goals of today's investor are not really different from those in past: the first is the *preservation of capital* and the second is the *creation of wealth*.

Preservation of Capital

The preservation of capital involves the protection of one's assets from depreciation over time, that is, maintaining the value or purchasing power of one's investments. Depreciation can result from either an outright decline in the value of investments, or from a failure to keep pace with taxation and prevailing economic conditions such as inflation. Stock market fluctuations often severely impair the individual investor's ability to preserve capital. As noted in Chapter 1, because of buy-and-hold strategies that do not include selling short in down markets, not only did the Dow Jones Industrial Average decline from 1,000 in 1972 to a low of about 680 in 1975—a loss of over 30 percent—but even after the market had rebounded in 1982, the real value of the Dow when adjusted for inflation over that period had declined to well under 300, or to a value similar to that during the Great Depression in 1929.

Even such stock market stalwarts as IBM have been known to lose 50 percent or more of their market value during bear markets. This raises the issue of the relative risks to the preservation of capital of a variety of different types of investments. You normally wouldn't consider IBM to be a "risky" investment. Still, most investors have somehow assumed, quite incorrectly, that commodity futures carry a degree of risk inherently greater than that of equity investments. This misconception has been caused, in part, by investors' general lack of understanding of the various approaches to the futures markets. Approached conservatively, the average volatility of futures prices can be less than that of securities.

Indepth research by leading investment analysts Zvi Bodie and Victor I. Rosansky, as used by Commodities Corporation officials Jack Barbanel, Phil Lipsky, and John Zumbrunn (*Futures,* December 1983) reveals that an investment index of futures can be developed similar to stock or bond indexes such as Standard & Poor's (S&P) 500 stock index. This enables the investor to compare relative risks and rates of return for stocks, bonds, bills, and commodity futures.

As indicated in Table 2-1, a portfolio comprising a mix of 25 percent futures, 25 percent stocks, and 50 percent T-bills has carried no more risk than a traditionally conservative portfolio of 20 percent stocks and 80 percent T-bills. Yet, as Table 2-1 shows, the portfolio including commodity futures clearly outperformed the portfolio containing only stocks and T-bills by 160 basis points (8.0% vs. 6.4%).

The Creation of Wealth

Now consider the investor's second fundamental goal: the creation of wealth.

Investors are concerned with increasing the value of their assets, that is, with increasing the rate of return on investments. Once again, the returns of the commodity futures index outperformed those of stocks, bonds, and T-bills over the entire 22-year period (Mean Return, Table 2-3), as did the portfolios containing futures in their asset mix (Effective Annual Return, Table 2-1).

If we examine the rates of return for major investment areas in Table 2-3 for the years 1960-1982, we will note that returns on the S&P 500 index were negative in seven years, and the returns on government bonds were negative in eight years, whereas the returns on the commodity futures index were negative in only four years.

A closer look reveals that the commodity futures index increased in six of the seven years that the S&P stock index declined in value, and in all eight years that the government bonds declined in value. This is one of several indications of a high degree of negative correlation between stocks and commodity futures, and between bonds and commodity futures. Thus, in periods of declining stock and bond prices,

Table 2–1
Returns of Various Mixes with a 5 Percent Risk of Losing Any Principal
(Percent in Portfolios)

Portfolio Mix	Commodities	S & P 500	Long–Term Bonds	T-Bills	Effective Annual Return
1.	0	20	0	80	6.4
2.	30	15	5	50	7.9
3.	25	25	5	45	7.9
4.	25	25	0	50	8.0

Source: Barbanel, Lipsky, Zumbrunn, "Why Futures Belong in Institutional Portfolios," *Futures,* December 1983.

Table 2–2
Correlation Matrix of Annual Rates of Return
(1960–1982)

	Commodities	S&P 500	Bonds	T-Bills
Commodities	1.000	–0.411	–0.185	0.091
S&P 500	–0.411	1.000	0.021	–0.152
Long-term bonds	–0.185	0.021	1.000	–0.274
T-bills	0.091	–0.152	–0.274	1.000

Source: Barbanel, Lipsky, Zumbrunn, "Why Futures Belong in Institutional Portfolios," *Futures,* December 1983.

Table 2–3
Rates of Return for Major Investment Areas
(Annual Percentage Rates)

Year	Indexed Commodities	S&P 500	Government Bonds	T-Bills
1960	−0.2	0.5	13.8	2.6
1961	3.3	26.9	1.0	2.2
1962	7.0	−8.7	6.9	2.7
1963	30.2	22.8	1.2	3.2
1964	−15.4	16.5	3.5	3.5
1965	12.8	12.5	0.7	3.9
1966	6.4	−10.1	3.6	4.8
1967	6.6	24.0	−9.2	4.2
1968	6.8	11.1	−0.3	5.2
1969	8.4	−8.5	−5.1	6.6
1970	5.8	4.0	12.1	6.5
1971	11.3	14.3	13.2	4.4
1972	21.3	19.0	5.7	3.8
1973	63.3	−14.7	−1.1	6.9
1974	47.3	−26.5	4.4	8.0
1975	−11.7	37.2	9.2	5.8
1976	6.7	23.8	16.7	5.1
1977	7.0	−7.2	−0.7	5.1
1978	15.2	6.6	−1.2	7.2
1979	32.1	18.4	−1.2	10.4
1980	1.1	32.4	−3.9	11.3
1981	−7.6	−5.0	1.8	13.6
1982	6.0	21.4	40.4	10.5
Mean return	11.71	8.71	3.24	5.77
Standard deviation	17.17	17.65	6.52	2.89
Mean return divided by standard deviation	0.682	0.493	0.497	1.999

Source: Barbanel, Lipsky, Zumbrunn, "Why Futures Belong in Institutional Portfolios," *Futures,* December 1983.

Table 2–4
Returns from Portfolios with Commodities
(Annual Percentage Returns)

Year	Portfolio Mix				Mean Return	Actual Return	Perfect Knowledge (Constant Mix)
	Commod-ities	Stocks	Bonds	T-Bills			
1965	5	40	55	0	7.9	6.0	8.3
1966	5	45	50	0	7.9	−2.4	1.5
1967	15	25	60	0	5.8	1.5	9.8
1968	10	25	25	40	5.3	5.4	7.0
1969	10	25	15	50	5.5	1.2	3.3
1970	10	20	0	70	5.1	6.0	5.7
1971	15	20	0	65	5.3	7.4	8.6
1972	10	25	0	65	5.6	9.4	12.0
1973	15	25	5	55	6.1	9.6	15.6
1974	20	25	0	55	6.7	7.2	9.2
1975	25	15	0	60	7.2	6.1	9.3
1976	25	25	0	50	7.4	10.2	10.2
1977	30	25	0	45	8.0	2.6	2.5
1978	25	25	0	50	7.3	9.0	9.0
1979	30	25	0	45	7.8	18.9	17.8
1980	25	25	0	50	7.9	14.0	14.0
1981	30	25	5	40	8.5	2.0	3.6
1982	25	25	0	50	8.0	12.1	12.1

Summary 1970–1982

	Stocks	Bonds	Half Stocks & Half Bonds	T-Bills	"Naive" Allocator
Effective rate	7.9%	6.8%	7.8%	7.5%	8.7%
Losing years	4	5	4	0	0

Source: Barbanel, Lipsky, and Zumbrunn, "Why Futures Belong in Institutional Portfolios," *Futures,* December 1983.

Tables 2–1 through 2–4 show a startling conclusion: a portfolio comprising a mix of futures, stocks, and T-bills carries no more risk than a portfolio with only stocks and T-bills, but the former portfolio clearly outperforms the latter. (See particularly Table 2–1.)

Table 2–5
Commodity Futures Versus Common Stocks As Inflation Hedges

Seven Years of Greatest Acceleration in Inflation*	Commodity Futures		Common Stocks	
	Best Seven Years	Worst Seven Years	Best Seven Years	Worst Seven Years
1950	1950	1952	1954	1953
1956	1951	1953	1958	1957
1966	1963	1955	1961	1962
1968	1969	1957	1963	1966
1969	1972	1958	1967	1969
1973	1973	1960	1972	1973
1974	1974	1975	1975	1974

*Acceleration of inflation is measured as the increase in the rate of inflation over the previous year's rate.

Source: Bodie and Rosansky, "Risk and Return in Commodity Futures," *Financial Analysts Journal*, May-June 1980.

an offsetting mix of assets in futures can not only reduce the downside risk in a mixed portfolio, thereby helping to preserve capital; it can also increase overall portfolio returns, thereby creating additional wealth for the investor. And it does this in a risk adjusted way that is less volatile than stocks and bonds (mean return divided by standard deviation, Table 2–3).

Inflation Hedges

As a hedge against accelerating inflation, commodity futures have been shown to be far superior to common stocks. Table 2–5 (page 23), developed by Zvi Bodie and Victor I. Rosansky, lists the seven years of greatest acceleration in the rate of inflation for the 25-year period 1950–1975 and compares the best and worst seven years for indices of commodity futures and common stocks during that same period.

As you can see, four of the seven worst inflation years turned out to be years showing the best performance in commodity futures (1950, 1969, 1973, 1974), while four of the inflation years turned up big losers for stocks (1966, 1969, 1973, 1974). In addition, the inflation years represent those years with the greatest increase in the rate of inflation over the previous year's rate—an indication that the accelerated rate of inflation was largely unanticipated by many investors, both professional and amateur.

Risk-Return Tradeoff Curves

As we have indicated, commodity futures can produce higher overall portfolio returns at a lower level of risk when included in a diversified investment portfolio. Figure 2–1 shows the risk-return curves for two portfolios: one composed of stocks, bonds, and bills (1), and the other of stocks,

Figure 2–1
Risk-Return Tradeoff Curves

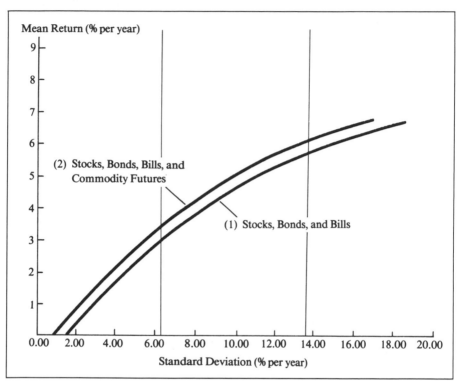

Source: Zvi Bodie, "Commodity Futures As a Hedge against Inflation," *The Journal of Portfolio Management,* Spring 1983.

This figure compares the risk-return on a portfolio composed of stocks, bonds, and bills with one composed of stocks, bonds, bills, and commodity futures.

bonds, bills, *and commodity futures* (2). The *standard deviation* is a measure of volatility (risk) in the portfolio. The portfolio including commodity futures not only produces greater returns at the same level of risk, but also produces equivalent returns at a lower level of risk—just what is wanted by rational investors.

A Sample Portfolio

What kind of portfolio mix will most likely meet your investment objectives in today's uncertain investment climate? Every investor has individual preferences regarding short-, mid-, and long-term goals. Consider a typical portfolio composed of the following investments:

30 percent in bonds.
20 percent in cash or cash equivalents.
35 percent in stocks.
15 percent in real estate investments and other shelters.

100 percent

Given these basic investments, we can begin to construct a portfolio that includes commodity futures. This new portfolio includes 25 percent invested in commodity futures. A new asset mix can be achieved without any major disruption to the existing portfolio. A reasonable reduction in each of the assets previously invested in bonds, cash (and cash equivalents), and stocks produces a revised asset mix of 15 percent real estate/shelters, 30 percent stocks, 25 percent commodity futures, 20 percent bonds, and 10 percent cash. This revised portfolio can produce significantly higher gains while reducing overall portfolio risk under a variety of economic and market conditions.

Sample Portfolio Construction

	Existing	Revised
Bonds	30%	20%
Cash and cash equivalents	20	10
Stocks	35	30
Real estate/shelters	15	15
Futures	0	25
Total	100%	100%

Personal Portfolio Construction

	Existing	Revised
Bonds		20%
Cash and cash equivalents		10
Stocks		30
Real estate/shelters		15
Futures		25
Total		100%

The personal portfolio construction table above allows you to compare your own existing portfolio to the sample portfolio recommended by the authors.

Comparison of Commodity Futures with Alternative Investments

Commodity futures offer alternatives to traditional investments, and have their own unique characteristics. A comparison of these characteristics with those of other investment instruments demonstrates why commodity futures offer the profit and risk management potentials desired by more conservative investors.

Shares of common stock, for instance, have no particular value directly related to *time*. They are, in a sense, timeless. Shares of stock have no expiration date. This is one reason why stocks are more applicable to an investor's "buy-and-hold" tendencies. The passive "buy-and-hold" strategy of so many stock investors developed during the recovery from the 1930s Depression and lasted through the post-war growth of the 1940s and 1950s, and the economic expansion of the 1960s and early 1970s. Only recently has this approach begun to yield to more realistic and actively managed investment approaches—and with good reason. For example, if you bought IBM at its peak price in 1973, you would have had to wait nine years just to get your money back. Look at the opportunity cost you paid.

Futures, on the other hand, have a definite lifespan. Each futures contract has an expiration month and day after which the contract ceases to exist. Most futures contracts have a lifetime of less than 18 months. Therefore, one element of any futures contract's value is related to the time remaining before its expiration. Consequently, a different kind of investment psychology exists in the futures markets.

While a "buy-and-hold" approach to futures can be, under certain market conditions, prudent, it is usually more prudent to use discipline and quickly realize relatively smaller losses than it is to sit with a losing position waiting for it to recover. When the losing contract is closed out, new positions having better profit potential can be opened. Actively managing the account to limit losses is the more risk averse and opportunistic investment strategy, expressing a "buy-and-sell" psychology, quite different from the traditional "buy-and-hold" stock market psychology.

Another major difference that should be noted by the investor considering the futures markets—one that at first makes some investors uneasy—is that profits can be made in the futures markets whether prices are going up or down.

When you buy stock, you hope that the market value of that stock goes up. If the stock price goes up you can profit. But if the stock price declines you lose money. Of course, more sophisticated stock strategies have been developed to enable investors to profit from declining stock prices, including the sale of short stock or the use of stock options. But for 95 percent of investors who buy stocks, the profit potential is tied to rising stock prices while declining stock prices represent the downside risk.

In the futures markets, however, profits are routinely taken in times of both declining and rising prices. Short selling in commodities has none of the negative connotations that it has in stock market investing. In fact, more money has been made in the last few years from the downward movement of many commodity prices (e.g., of grains, tropical foods, precious metals, foreign currencies, and energy futures).

The important consideration for investors is simply that declining commodity prices do not necessarily represent pure risk as it often does with stock ownership.

The *trending* nature of commodity futures markets makes these markets a highly fertile field for the investor's profit potential. Relatively long-term *major trends*—up and down—are a primary characteristic of the futures markets. The astute investor, trader, or futures portfolio manager can profit during the developing portion of any such major trend.

Fundamental Features of Commodity Futures

It may be useful to describe some of the fundamental features of commodity futures before we discuss in detail the role that they can play to enhance portfolio returns and reduce investment risk.

Commodities futures are financial instruments in the form of contracts. A futures contract is a contract to buy or sell a standardized item—gold in troy ounces, oil in gallons, cocoa in tons, oats in bushels, T-bonds in dollars, etc.—at some specified date. These contracts are traded (bought and sold) on federally regulated exchanges. The largest of these exchanges are the Chicago Board of Trade and the Chicago Mercantile Exchange, which together account for approximately 74 percent of all futures trading.

Futures contracts, in and of themselves, have monetary value, influenced by but not totally bound to the delivered price (also referred to as "spot" or cash price) of the underlying commodity; that is, the price that the buyer must pay for the actual "physical" commodity represented by the futures contract. Price values for the futures contracts are established through a process of open outcry—competitive bidding, buying and selling during set trading hours. The "organized," highly specialized frenzy of the exchange floor where prices are bid, up and down, is an example of pure capitalism and price discovery as established by the marketplace that every investor should observe at least once.

Among the major futures markets are included those in

wheat, corn, soybeans, soybean oil and meal, pork bellies, live cattle, feeder cattle, and hogs as well as coffee, cocoa, sugar, cotton, heating oil, lumber, and precious metals such as gold and silver.

Futures are also traded on currencies including the Swiss franc, the West German deutsche mark, the British pound, the Japanese yen, and the Canadian dollar. And they are traded on interest rate instruments such as Treasury bills, Treasury bonds, and GNMAs.

The most significant recent additions to the futures markets are futures contracts on broad-based stock indexes including the Standard & Poor's 500 Index, the Value Line Index, the New York Stock Exchange Composite Index, and the Major Market Index.

Those less familiar with futures markets should note that most futures trading is done in advance of delivery dates for the underlying commodity and that less than 3 percent of all futures contracts are actually ever delivered.

Margin Requirements

Both futures and stock markets share the concept of initial and maintenance margins. But there are major differences—and, we believe, major advantages for the investor in futures.

An investor purchasing stocks on margin puts up a partial payment for the stock and borrows the balance from the broker. The purchased stock collateralizes the loan and the investor is charged interest on the loan balance by the brokerage firm.

When an investor fulfills a margin requirement for a futures contract, the transaction does not represent the purchase of the contract, nor a partial payment—rather, it is a *good faith deposit, a performance bond against the execu-*

tion of the contract. No interest payments are required since in effect no loan has been made.

Minimum initial margin requirements for futures contracts are set by the exchanges. Generally, the minimum initial margin requirement will range between 5 and 15 percent of the fully delivered price of the contract. The requirements are not fixed, however, and may be increased or decreased by the exchanges periodically, depending upon price volatility and market conditions. While the initial margin requirements are set by the exchanges, brokerage firms and/or clearing members may require margins above the posted exchange minimums.

Because futures are acquired on margin, the investor—whether as buyer or seller—commands assets many times greater than the cash or cash equivalents securing the contract. The financial leverage can therefore be substantial.

The risk and reward characteristics of futures investing should always be considered in light of this leverage, which represents both the investor's potential reward, as well as his or her liability. Keeping this in mind, it's little wonder that of the many non-professionals who try their hand at futures trading, more than 65 percent end up in the loss column.

In Chapter 4 we will discuss conservative investment strategies that use cash management approaches that have effectively eliminated the need for an investor to get a margin call. For now, let us say that a margin call may be the first sign of a losing strategy.

Chapter 3

Jumping In: Which Way Should I Go?

Evaluating commodity investment strategies.

Public commodity funds, private commodity pools, and individually managed futures accounts: Which is best?

A variety of methods and strategies are available to the investor seeking to utilize the futures markets in pursuit of more sophisticated risk management and higher portfolio returns. This chapter examines three broad categories of such strategies. The first can be called a long-term buy-and-hold approach to commodity futures investing. This strategy is based on research conducted by Zvi Bodie (see the discussion of an index of futures in Chapter 2). The second is a self-directed or self-managed approach to commodity futures investing. The third is a professionally managed approach, along with several options available to the investor who would look to a professional futures money manager.

Long Term Buy and Hold

Based on the approach developed by Bodie and Rosansky in "Risk and Return in Commodity Futures,"[1] and utilized by

[1]Bodie and Rosansky, "Risk and Return in Commodity Futures", *Financial Analysts Journal*, May-June 1980.

Barbanel, Lipsky, and Zumbrunn in the development of their commodity futures index (see Chapter 2), a long-term buy-and-hold approach to futures involves the maintenance of long futures positions in a diversified mix of commodities. Such commodities could include metals, grains, meats, currencies, and interest rate futures. They would be margined at 100 percent (full contract price paid at the opening of the position) to create a smoother and less volatile fluctuation without the magnified effect of leverage as the price changes, similar to the way most people invest in stocks without margins. As we have seen, this strategy can be an effective means of achieving a more level risk curve with an equity-based portfolio—particularly during extended inflationary periods such as the 1970s, when inflation helped to sustain a prolonged bull market in many commodities and the stock market suffered an extended retreat.

The obvious advantages of such a passive investment approach during prolonged inflationary periods would, clearly, not apply at other times. The relative deflationary forces which helped create a rebound in most stock prices in the early 1980s have tended to correlate negatively with most commodity prices, making the strategy highly ineffective.

Therein lies one of the major disadvantages with a long-term strategy based on a continuous equity stream in long futures positions. One may be able to liquidate those positions at the right time, but such a strategy would require a careful monitoring by the investor during these periods.

Similarly, this strategy would be excessively dependent on the existence of extremely long-term trends, fueled by larger inflationary forces in the economy and maintained by similar monetary policies for extended periods.

In the absence of extended inflationary trends, an investor attempting to employ such a naive strategy in the commodity markets would be at the mercy of either a long-term reversal of such trends or, more likely, wide intermediate-term equity swings which would significantly strain any conservative investor's confidence—not to mention the strains on his capital. For this reason alone, this approach is not recommended by the authors.

The Self-Managed Approach

Another alternative, favored by some heartier types, is the investor's self-management of futures investing. In this approach an investor makes his or her own decisions regarding futures trading, utilizing a broker strictly for the execution and clearing of trades.

Such a self-directed approach should only be considered by an investor willing to devote large amounts of time and capital to the futures market, who is willing to assume and withstand a high degree of risk, and who is experienced in the trading of futures.

For the traditional equity investor, this approach would require obtaining highly specialized knowledge of an array of futures—as many as 40 different markets—as well as the experience of trading in these markets under a variety of cyclical market conditions. Unfortunately, statistics indicate that anywhere from 65 to 90 percent of public investors—even those with some experience—who attempt to direct their own futures programs turn up losers in the futures markets. And considering the degree to which individual positions are leveraged, losses here can be substantial.

The Professionally Managed Approach

For the overwhelming majority of investors seeking to diversify their standard equity-based portfolios by investing in futures, a better alternative is to be found among the professionally managed programs. These are designed to provide the investor with the kind of expertise in the futures markets that he or she may already be utilizing in other markets.

There are three major forms of professional futures management—public commodity funds, private commodity pools, and individually managed futures accounts—all of which employ the services of registered and professional money managers called Commodity Trading Advisors. (In Chapter 6, we will examine in some detail the roles played by these investment professionals in managed accounts.)

Public Commodity Funds

Today, many brokerage firms and wirehouses offer investors a way of participating in the futures markets through public commodity funds. These funds, registered as public offerings with the Securities and Exchange Commission and the Commodity Futures Trading Commission, are similar in many respects to mutual funds offered in the equities markets. They usually take the form of a limited partnership, and are issued to the public through the sale of participatory units in a commingled fund. Units often require a modest capital cost, ranging anywhere from $2,000 to as much as $25,000, depending on the particular fund.

The value of the units fluctuates in accordance with the relative performance of the fund as a whole as well as with the relative demand for the units among public investors. In most cases, sales charges and management fees will be deducted, but because the investor's equity is in the form of units in the fund and not in the form of futures contracts directly, the investor will be risking only the capital invested in the participatory units. Investors in such funds generally realize profits through dividend payouts, if offered by the specific fund, or through the sale of units as they appreciate. Such public funds usually charge a management fee to participants in the fund, regardless of fund performance.

Private Commodity Pools

Another form of professionally managed futures investment, widely known as private commodity pools, is similar in some respects to the public funds. They are normally offered in the form of private placements, usually with significantly higher per-unit minimums than those required for public funds. As with the funds, sales commissions, offering expenses and ongoing administrative fees are incurred.

In most cases, commodity pools are closed-end private placements, with investment funds commingled and management fees assessed. Because they are *private*, rather than public funds, less information will often be available to the investor, depending, in part, on the degree of state regulatory requirements. Liquidity can be a serious problem for many pool investors, including investors in public funds, because of contractual arrangements that lock them in for varying periods of time. In general, the investor depends on the general partner and can do little to influence the fund on his or her own behalf.

Funds and Pools: Some Specific Problems

Both public funds and private pools are formalized, commingled investment vehicles. Your capital is combined with the capital of others; therefore, your abililty to influence the success of the investment and the opportunity to personalize it to your needs does not exist. In most cases, your only

representative is an account executive from a stock brokerage firm whose knowledge about commodity futures is generally limited. This is not the best arrangement for investors
whose knowledge of futures is also limited.

Specific problems with funds and pools include:

Performance: Funds have historically achieved results that are
approximately one-half of the results achieved by well-
managed individual accounts.

Profit distributions: The senior management of funds and
pools determines profit distribution. Your personal requirements are not the basis of these decisions.

Upfront costs: Sales commissions, administrative fees, and
other offering expenses reduce the amount of capital that is
actually invested in these vehicles.

Ongoing costs: These further reduce profits.

T-bill interest: Interest earned on short-term T-bills—which
are used by the funds and pools as cash equivalents to secure
margin requirements—is usually not distributed to the investor but rather goes to management for a period of time,
until initial expenses are recovered. The investor is thus de-
prived of the additional interest income.

Poor management design: In many cases, only one trading advisor is involved, thus foregoing the risk-reduction provided
by the diversification of complementary trading systems as
practiced by two different trading advisors. In addition, the
investor has no power to remove an advisor who performs
poorly.

Individually Managed Futures Accounts: The Recommended Approach

In light of the preceding discussion of the negative aspects
of funds and pools, and considering the unique advantages

of individually managed futures accounts, the authors recommend the latter approach.

Of the three types of professionally managed commodity futures investments, only individually managed futures accounts are tailor-made for the serious individual investor. As such they usually require a higher level of capitalization—often a $50,000 minimum. Yet for many investors with existing investment portfolios valued at $500,000 or more, that kind of capital commitment provides precisely the kind of asset mix which can help to diversify the risks inherent in other markets and investments.

The funds held in a managed futures account are not commingled with those of other investors, as is the case with both commodity pools and public funds. The managed futures account is under the supervision of a professional money manager called a trading advisor who will personally decide on the futures positions in the account as well as determine which portion of the account will be invested or held in cash. A portion of the account's equity is usually in the form of short-term Treasury bills (30–90 days), a unique feature of commodity investing which provides the investor with *additional* income in the form of interest on the T-bills. Simultaneously, these funds can also be invested in futures contracts.

As shall be described in detail in forthcoming chapters, each trading advisor, acting as the investor's portfolio or money manager, will have a preferred style, trading philosophy, and set of strategies. Finding the trading advisor best suited to individual investment goals and individual perceptions of risks and potential rewards can be a difficult task. In some cases, an individual investor's knowledge of available trading advisors will depend on the advisor's public visibility. In other cases, the investor may be able to obtain referrals from commodity brokerage firms. All operating commodity trading advisors must be registered with the

Commodity Futures Trading Commission and must offer a modified prospectus, called a "Disclosure Document" to prospective investors.

Still, for an investor unfamiliar with the futures markets and the various types of potential trading strategies, accurately assessing available information can be difficult. One trading advisor may be right for an investor, while another, with similar credentials and equal levels of performance, may be unsuitable.

Some investment firms presently offer a variety of services to assist the individual investor with the process of finding, researching, assessing, and monitoring trading advisors so that the best match can be made between investor and trading advisor. In addition to providing such research, referral, and selection services, several firms also *manage the manager*—generating daily management reports on the status of the investor's account and monitoring the performance of the account's trading advisor. This helps to ensure that the account is managed so as to best meet the individual investor's overall goals.

For the serious investor generally lacking the time and/or experience in the futures markets, the array of services offered through a professionally managed individual futures account—including daily monitoring, supervision of trading advisors, and close scrutiny of the markets—has proven the best possible alternative to direct personal involvement and less disciplined approaches.

Chapter
4

Winners Versus Losers

A profile of a successful investing approach.
Why investors lose money in commodities.
The important differences in our winning approach.

Although short, this chapter could well be the most valuable one since these principles of successful investing apply to *all* your investments. Use it as a benchmark against which to evaluate present and proposed investments—and the chance of your being successful will be greatly enhanced.

It is estimated that anywhere from 65 to 90 percent of individual speculators in the commodity futures markets end up losing money. Why is this? And, more importantly, why do the winners win? What distinguishes the winners from the losers—besides the fact that winners realize consistent, attractive returns on their investments?

Before choosing the investment path to follow in the commodity futures market, the investor needs to examine the critical factors leading to success or failure in futures investing. We have constructed a chart that quickly shows the differences in approach taken by losers and winners. The chart applies to stock market investing as well as it applies to commodities. The chart has gained wide atten-

Table 4–1
Winners and Losers
Critical Factors in Determining Success or Failure in Futures Investing

Investment Factors	Loser	Winner
Capitalization	Undercapitalized; can absorb few losses; cannot lessen risks by diversifying	Well capitalized—can absorb reasonable losses while diversified profits develop
Capital Management	Usually 100 percent invested	Maintains large, long–term reserves
Discipline	Emotional; takes big losses, small profits	Reacts to preset buy/sell signals
Planned Strategy	Little planning; changing strategy; frequently averages down on positions	Limits losing positions; never averages down; cuts losses, lets profits run
Expertise	Little market knowledge	Is an expert—and uses experts
Diversification	Builds concentrated, single positions	Trades 15 to 25 different markets; never more than 10 percent in one market
Latest Information	Imperfect knowledge	Well–tested trading systems, research
Goals	Instant gratification	Long–term plan
Risk Control	Often none; frequently wiped out; takes high risks	Uses alerts, protective–stop points; if equity drops to a certain point, trading ceases

Table 4–1 *Continued*

Investment Factors	Loser	Winner
Timing	Decisions made only when broker calls; gets news too late	Acts immediately upon signals and market knowledge
Margin Calls	Very frequent	Never
Attention to Market	Part–time attention, misses data, trends	Full–time following of market prices, trends
Investor Contact	Infrequent, and rare in adverse markets	Regular, frequent contact—in all market conditions

This table, constructed by the authors, will help you in making investments in all markets. It may also be used to evaluate investments and prospective investment managers.

tion in the investment world, and has been reprinted in *Forbes* and several other publications. The chart, as originally developed by us, is reproduced in Table 4–1. Let's look at some of the critical factors revealed in it.

In managing their investments, those who lose money are most often undercapitalized and overinvested in the market. The winners, on the other hand, in addition to being well capitalized, take a more conservative approach. They maintain sizeable cash reserves to reduce volatility, allow for greater diversification, and prevent margin calls for additional funds.

Discipline is crucial for sound, successful investing. Winners in the futures markets will utilize a variety of predetermined buy or sell signals, including the use of protective-stop points to limit risks and losses. Losers react emotionally, often running up big losses and only small profits on their positions. Winners are often highly diversified in the commodities markets, and will take small losses quickly while allowing profits to run. Losers experience frequent margin calls, which require the investor to provide additional cash, while successful commodities investors do not.

Primarily, winners distinguish themselves by having a highly professional level of expertise themselves, *or* available to them, and by taking a conservative approach determined by a long-term plan. Winners seek realistic returns on their invested capital over longer periods of time, while losers are often part-time amateurs, "taking shots" in the marketplace in search of instant gratification and a "fast million." They lose because they are emotional and take risks that the intelligent investor would find unacceptable. Winners limit their risks and utilize time-tested, successful trading systems while actively following the markets on a strictly full-time basis.

Fundamentally, then, to be a winner in the futures markets you need to follow the example of the winner's performance. You must either be a full-time futures professional with long successful experience in these markets, *or* you must invest your money with someone who is. You must take the conservative, risk-averse approach described in the chart, or use the services of a professional who does.

Which way should you go? In Chapter 5, we explain why we recommend the individual professionally managed commodity futures account program for today's investor.

Chapter

5

The Superiority of Professionally Managed Accounts

The best approach for today's investor is the individual, professionally managed commodity futures account.
It offers reduced costs, superior management, and greater returns with less risk.
Three major components of a managed futures account.
Actual results.
Further comparisons with stocks and bonds.

The design and management of private pools and public funds should be examined closely by anyone contemplating investing in them. As we have discussed in the previous chapter, large public funds are often poorly designed and, overall, have performed unevenly. And both pools and funds can fall short when it comes to the high level of liquidity desired by many investors.

In both cases, the risk/reward characteristics of pools and funds are, we believe, less attractive to those of the individually managed futures account.

Advantages of Individual Managed Accounts

Among the major advantages offered by the individual, professionally managed commodity futures account program are the following:

Consistently attractive annual returns of 30 to 40 percent, even after fees and commissions. These are published and documented pre-tax returns.

Accounts receive favorable tax treatment, a maximum of 32 percent.

The investor's capital is liquid; in most cases, the account can be completely liquidated and funds made available to the investor within 24 hours.

The account is traded by a full-time professional money manager, registered with the Commodity Futures Trading Commission as a commodity trading advisor (CTA), with years of successful performance records under a variety of economic and market conditions, i.e., recession, deflation, inflation, and high interest rates.

Performance-based compensation for trading advisors means that the trading advisor makes most of his money only if the client's account makes money.

Trading advisor invests his or her money in the same program as the client.

Improves the risk/reward characteristics of other investment holdings.

There are no upfront sales commissions deducted from the account.

Funds are separately managed.

When established through a leading, full-service futures brokerage firm, the trading advisor is carefully selected and monitored by a full-time account manager and other specialists acting strictly on the investor's behalf.

Major money center banks hold invested capital in customer-segregated accounts. There is no pooling of funds and the invested funds may not be used for operating expenses of the firm.

Most have cut-off points. Should equity fall one-third to one-half, trading ceases and the remainder of the funds are returned to the client.

The Three Major Components of a
Managed Futures Account

Figure 5–1 describes the flow of account management for what we consider an ideal individual, professionally managed, futures account program.

Figure 5–1
Three Major Components of the Managed Futures Account

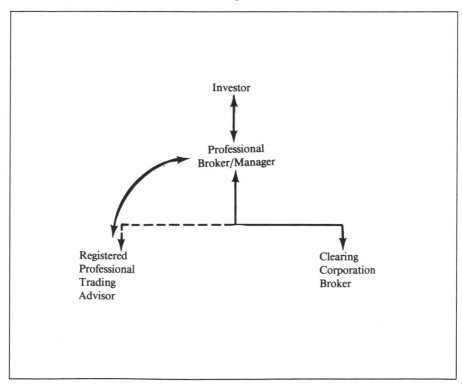

Figure 5-1
Three Major Components of the Managed Futures Account, *Concluded*

Broker Manager (Management Supervision)

Generally associated with a clearing member of an established exchange, the broker-manager provides a variety of valuable services for the investor. These include assisting the investor in finding the right trading advisor, close scrutiny of the investor's account (including daily reviews of the trading advisor's activity on behalf of the investor) and a broad-based market perspective. The broker-manager's duties are akin to those of a financial advisor or General Partner, though geared to the highly specialized futures markets. (In Chapter 12, we discuss in detail the role of the broker-manager.)

Registered Professional Trading Advisors (Money Management)

Trading advisors are usually referred to as Commodity Trading Advisors, or CTAs. Commodity Trading Advisors are responsible for establishing the accounts' trading and cash management strategies. They initiate trades which are then executed and cleared through the Clearing Corporation Broker. In general, they are most closely akin in their duties to portfolio managers or money managers in the securities markets. (In Chapters 6 and 7 we discuss in greater detail the role CTAs play in the managed account.)

Clearing Corporation Broker (Broker Execution and Administration)

The Clearing Corporation Broker is a clearing member of an exchange, and is responsible for the quality execution of brokerage transactions; that is, ensuring the best prices both entering and exiting the market. (In Chapter 13, we describe what the investor should look for and expect from the Clearing Corporation Broker.)

The investor establishes the account through a professional broker-manager who is affiliated with a leading futures brokerage firm, which also serves as the broker and clearing corporation for transactions conducted in the account. The investor works directly with the firm's broker-manager to select the best independent, outside money manager to serve as the trading advisor for the account. Futures positions are determined by the trading advisor; overall supervision of the account is the responsibility of the firm's broker-manager. Regular contact is maintained with the investor by the broker-manager who in turn monitors all account activity on a daily basis.

Quality execution of trades—getting the best price entering and exiting the market—is assured by the brokerage firm, which also is responsible through its broker-manager for ensuring that investment and trading strategies, previously determined in discussions between the client and the money manager, are followed. Investors are relieved of the burden of making trading decisions, and their interests are defended by the broker-manager as well as by the incentive fee arrangement with the trading advisor. If at any time the investor or the broker-manager feel that the interests of the client would be better served by a new trading advisor, the entire account can be easily and conveniently moved.

A Superior Investment Vehicle

Why do individual managed accounts represent an investment vehicle superior to commodity pools or public funds for most of today's investors?

First, consider the front-end costs of various investments. Initial offering expenses, fees and sales commissions for pools and funds tend to cut into the potential profitability of these vehicles. This is particularly the case with up-front load and initiation costs. While management, incentive fees, and commission charges tend to average out evenly among pools, funds, and managed accounts, both pools and funds charge 10 to 15 percent of invested capital as a front-end expense. There are generally no up-front initiation or load charges for individual managed accounts.

This means that an investor placing $50,000 in a public commodity fund will generally be charged 15 percent up front, and immediately find himself $7,500 behind at the start, with only $42,500 actually invested. If the same investor opens a managed account with the same amount of funds, his account would open with a net asset value of $50,000.

The commingled nature of pools and funds can also make them unattractive for those investors who require a high degree of liquidity and quick and easy access to profits.

Liquidity and the distribution of profits are important factors to consider in pools or funds, because gains in the value of participatory units are taxable on a year-end basis, whether or not they have been distributed to the investor. It is not uncommon for pool and fund managers to elect to plow profits back into the commingled fund or pool. This can result in a compound loss for the investor who has paid taxes on capital gains on undistributed profits in one year and has the value of units sink below year-end value in the next. Naturally, the tax basis is stepped up in that year, but the investor has suffered a loss nevertheless.

More importantly, the managers of pools and funds have not always proven themselves to be capable in the selection and supervision of tradings advisors. Industry experts feel that public fund directors tend to select money managers who are so conservative that they do not allow profits to run up substantially. Private pools, on the other hand, are often controlled by money managers who are too aggressive for most investors. As a result, public funds have shown lower profits at lower levels of risk, while private pools have generally outperformed public funds, yet with considerably higher volatility and far greater risk to principal.

The well-conceived managed futures account, on the other hand, should far outstrip the performance of most public funds, with minimal additional risk. Industry experts estimate that in 1984 the average annual return from public commodity funds was 10.7 percent, while private pools carved out average returns of about 20 percent (*Managed Account Reports*, January 1985.) This 20 percent return was matched by average annual composite returns from individual managed futures accounts, but achieved with significantly lower levels of risk.

In addition to superior performance, individually managed accounts also offer the advantages of a more personalized investment strategy implemented by full-time professionals, along with increased diversification made possible by higher levels of capitalization, and equally as important, daily account supervision.

Investor Liability

We feel that the only advantage of a public fund lies in the fact that the investor's units are registered as securities and therefore the liability is limited to the total amount of the investment. However, in practice, because of the professional management of the account, liability is also tightly controlled. Undertrading the account, avoiding margin

calls, limiting position losses, ensuring proper account diversification among a variety of commodities and commodity groups, and daily supervision by a group of specialists
are some of the methods used by successful managers to
limit risks and liabilities. Trading is usually stopped should
30 to 50 percent in losses be incurred. To the authors'
knowledge, investors participating in managed accounts in
the recommended way have not had calls for additional
funds nor experienced catastrophic losses.

Reward and Risk

Let us now look at examples of actual results achieved by
trading advisors in individually managed futures accounts
supervised by the authors. Throughout the book, these results are presented not only to show average annual rates of
return (reward), but also to show monthly fluctuations, for
these monthly fluctuations are indicative of the risk you
may experience. It is our contention that the actual risk-re-
ward ratios will be considered favorable even by very conservative investors. Later in this chapter we shall compare
these with the performance of stock and bond investing.

Leading Trading Advisors' Performance

For example, Table 5–1 lists the monthly and cumulative
one-year returns from an actual managed account with an
initial investment of $50,000. Despite relatively small,
short-term losses in five of the twelve months, this account
racked up a one-year return of 51.3 percent net profit to the
investor after fees and commissions. After one year, this
$50,000 account grew to a net asset value of $75,631.

Table 5–1
1984 Results of an Actual $50,000 Account
51 Percent Net to the Client

1984	Monthly Net Profits	Rate of Return	Cumulative Net Profits	Cumulative Return
January	$ 6,069	12.1%	$ 6,069	12.1%
February	(3,321)	−6.6	2,748	5.5
March	(3,163)	−6.3	(415)	−0.8
April	350	0.7	(65)	−0.1
May	5,625	11.2	5,560	11.1
June	(4,124)	−8.2	1,437	2.9
July	10,942	21.9	12,378	24.8
August	(296)	−0.6	12,082	24.2
September	8,982	18.0	21,064	42.1
October	403	0.8	21,468	42.9
November	(3,149)	−6.3	18,319	36.6
December	7,312	14.6	25,631	**51.3**

Net of all commissions and fees. Commissions charged averaged $70.

Table 5–2 lists the performance records, as published by *Managed Account Reports* of seven leading managed account trading advisors who have been selected by the authors at various times to trade individual managed futures accounts. The performances of these seven trading advisors are compared and averaged for annual rates of return on funds under management for each of the years 1980–83.

Further, out of 28 trading advisor years (seven advisors ×four years), 24 years were up and only four years were down—with the average annual rate of return for the four year period at 61 percent (1980–83).

Table 5–2
Performance Chart: Seven Leading Trading Advisors
Average Annual Rate of Return on Funds under Management (in Percent) 61%

Money Manager	1980	1981	1982	1983	Four Year Average	Cumulative
No. 1	149.9	33.3	25.1	24.5	58.2	232.8
No. 2	−0.1	24.7	29.4	55.2	27.3	109.2
No. 3	13.4	11.6	31.9	30.9	21.95	87.8
No. 4	52.1	−3.9	14.5	−9.5	13.3	53.2
No. 5	31.0	38.2	7.6	31.5	27.07	108.3
No. 6	645.8	187.9	49.0	45.5	232.05	928.2
No. 7	89.9	−26.8	77.5	51.3	47.97	191.9
Average	140.28	37.85	33.57	32.77		
Four year average annual return for all seven managers					61.11	

Source: *Managed Account Reports*. LJR, Inc., Suite 213, 5513 Twin Knolls, Columbia, MD 21045.

Table 5–3
Funds Average Performance
(Average Annual Rates of Return in Percent)

1980	1981	1982	1983	Four Year Average	Cumulative
40.8	19.0	0.5	−9.8	12.63	50.5

Source: *Quarterly Funds Report,* 1984–IV (Table V). LJR Inc., Suite 213, 5513 Twin Knolls, Columbia, MD 21045.

If we look at Table 5–3 which shows annual rates of return for a four-year period (1980–1983) for public commodity funds and compare these to Table 5–2, we can see that the four-year average annual rate of return of these public funds averaged only 12.63 percent throughout the same period during which the seven leading individual account trading advisors averaged 61.11 percent.

Further Comparisons with Stocks and Bonds

In the November 1984 issue of *Financial Planning*, Henry K. Clasing, Jr., in his article "The Mixing Blessing," compared the rates of returns for a variety of instruments—including a portfolio of 15 futures money managers. Covering a 42-month period (July 1979–December 1982), Clasing's study showed that the 15 futures money managers achieved a 32.9 percent annual return, while portfolios comprised of stocks and bonds achieved annual returns of 16.8 percent and 10.0 percent, respectively.

While the comparisons in this study indicate a dramatic difference between the performance of futures and stocks and bonds, of equal importance is Clasing's insight into the fact that price changes in the futures markets are not only independent of price activity in the securities markets but actually correlate negatively. Evidence of this negative correlation strongly suggests that futures can provide what Clasing calls an "insurance effect"—that is to say, futures can significantly improve the overall risk/reward characteristic of a stock and bond portfolio by providing protection when the overall security markets decline.

Clasing also presents in his article a table that was previously referred to in Chapter 2 of this book (Table 2–3) "Rates of Return for Major Investment Areas." In reviewing that table for 1960–1980 period, it should be noted that commodities had fewer down years than stocks and bonds, had a greater mean return *and* were less volatile. As Clasing himself concludes, managed futures accounts, when included in a portfolio of stocks and bonds, can enhance overall portfolio performance, significantly reducing downside risk, while improving returns.

Chapter
6

Money Management and Trading Approaches

Risk, return, and investment strategy.
Conservative versus aggressive trading systems.
Trend following.
Technical and fundamental analysis: Which is more successful?
Specialized trading approaches.
Actual trading advisor profiles.
What to look for in selecting a trading advisor.

Identifying the characteristics that distinguish one advisor from another is an important process. To do so, the investor needs to develop a measure by which to compare the relative risk and reward characteristics of different trading strategies, and techniques.

Weighing Risk and Reward Characteristics

One way to approach the question of the relative risk and reward characteristics of different trading advisors is to examine Figures 6–1 and 6–2. The results of the advisor represented in Figure 6–1 shows that he has an average return, shown by the vertical line labelled *arithmetic mean.* However, you can see that he has never actually achieved that return in reported results; sometimes he is below, and other times above. This variation shows that the average return may not accurately describe the actual return achieved by the advisor. Similarly, *average* rates of return can be the same for different managers with different risk characteris-

Figure 6–1

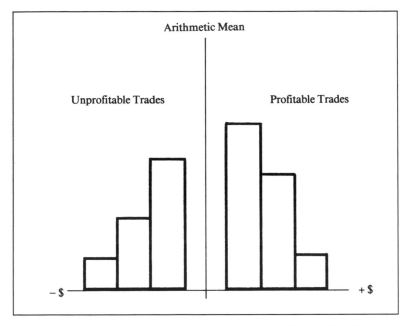

Source: Fred S. Gehm, "Analyzing Risk/Reward Tradeoffs," *Technical Analysis of Stocks & Commodities,* March–April 1984

Figure 6–1 shows the difference between the average return, shown by the arithmetic mean, and the actual return during a particular period.

tics. Figure 6–2 shows two managers generating the same average profit, but the returns of Manager B are achieved with three times the level of volatility of Manager A. A look at the horizontal axis reveals that Manager B takes greater losses as well as higher profits to achieve the same average return as Manager A. Manager A, therefore, maintains a

Figure 6–2

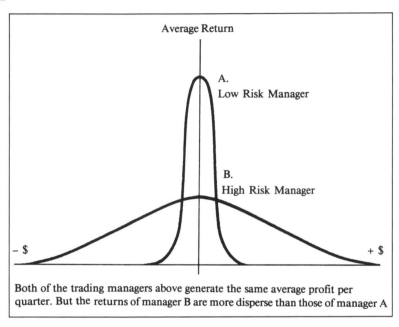

Both of the trading managers above generate the same average profit per quarter. But the returns of manager B are more disperse than those of manager A

Source: Fred S. Gehm, "Analyzing Risk/Reward Tradeoffs," *Technical Analysis of Stocks & Commodities,* March-April 1984.

In Figure 6–2, both of the trading managers generate the same average profit per quarter. But the returns of manager B are more disperse than those of manager A.

less volatile portfolio with less risk than Manager B for the same average rate of return.

The investor seeking a compatible trading advisor must become familiar with such comparisons of performance, or have someone else do so. Does the suitable trading advisor have a generally conservative approach, or a more aggressive one? Is the advisor more willing to assume a higher degree of potential risk in return for greater potential rewards? What level of downside risk is acceptable for the desired level of potential gain? In order to select the trading advisor who will best represent the investor's interest—his or her financial objectives and tolerance for risk—the investor should become familiar with the types of strategies and money management approaches the advisor follows.

General Characteristics of Trading Strategies

Although trading strategies often differ from one advisor to another, we can conveniently classify these strategies as conservative, aggressive, or middle-of-the-road. Each approach has its own risk/reward characteristics. Advisors who follow a conservative approach are willing to assume a 15 to 25 percent risk for brief periods of time in pursuit of annual returns of 25 to 35 percent on the upside. Aggressive advisors are willing to assume a higher degree of risk, in the range of 40 to 60 percent potential downside, in return for annual gains of 50 to 100 percent or more.

Most trading advisors, however, tend to fall somewhere in the middle, seeking returns of 30 to 50 percent while assuming a potential 25 to 35 percent risk for a brief period (three months in a one-and-a-half to two-year period). The most successful managers over long periods of time prove to be middle-of-the-road. They manage potential risks in the futures portfolio prudently while accumulating average annual pre-tax rates of return of 30 percent or more.

For example, Table 6–1 lists the composite monthly performance and rate of return of a trading advisor's one year performance. We can see that after the addition of $374,794, the account gained another $239,464, for an average annual

Table 6–1
Table of Composite Performance

Month	Beginning Net Asset Value	Additions	Net Performance	Ending Net Asset Value	Rate of Return (%)
January	504,360		69,131	573,491	13.7
February	573,491		(30,628)	542,863	(5.3)
March	542,863	24,794	38,266	605,923	7.0
April	605,923		(24,203)	581,720	(4.0)
May	581,720		65,597	647,317	11.3
June	647,317	350,000	(73,235)	924,082	(11.3)
July	924,083		(93,493)	830,589	(10.1)
August	830,589		105,885	936,474	12.7
September	936,474		39,167	975,641	4.2
October	975,641		145,469	1,121,110	14.9
November	1,121,110		2,226	1,123,336	0.2
December	1,123,336		(4,718)	1,118,618	(0.4)

Notes:

1. "Beginning Net Asset Value" represents the previous quarter's "Ending Net Asset Value."

2. "Additions" represents all additions to the account during the period.

3. "Net Performance" represents the change in Net Asset Value including "Additions" for the period.

4. "Ending Net Asset Value" equals the "Beginning Net Asset Value" plus or minus "Additions" and "Net Performance."

5. "Rate of Return" is calculated by dividing "Net Performance" by the "Beginning Net Asset Value" for the period.

return of 30.7 percent after fees and commissions. This significant level of performance was achieved despite the fact
that the account suffered short-term losses in five of the 12
months.

We are attempting to offer some basic measurements for
evaluating risk and reward ranges that are characteristic of a
variety of portfolio management approaches.

In addition to risk/reward considerations, however, there
are other key factors that determine whether a trading advisor's approach is aggressive or conservative. These include
the individual components of a trading system approach
such as the manager's approach to cash management, the
amount of position risk assumed and the degree or method
of diversification within the futures portfolio.

Cash Management

Cash management in a futures account involves the amount
of equity committed to specific futures positions as margin
requirements. For example, if a $100,000 managed futures
account has positions that require $40,000 in margin require-
ments, then we can say that the account is 40 percent margined at that particular time. The degree of margin in a managed account can vary greatly—but it usually ranges between
25 and 60 percent. The higher the degree of margin committed in the account, the more aggressive is the approach.

Position Risk

The degree of risk incurred by the manager while holding
futures positions can also vary and will tend to affect the
risk/reward characteristics of the account. Position risk involves a variety of factors, including the relative risks associated with the volatility of a particular commodity, the
number of futures contracts held of that commodity, and

the level of price fluctuation taken on specific trades. The prices of different commodities (e.g., pork bellies versus oats) can fluctuate to a greater or lesser degree and will therefore be more or less volatile, just as in the equity markets certain stocks such as utilities will be less volatile than many stocks of smaller high technology firms.

The degree of risk and portfolio volatility can be offset in a futures account by methods of diversification similar to those used in a stock portfolio, and the relative degree of diversification among a variety of commodities is also a reflection of the conservative or aggressive nature of the account and its manager.

Portfolio Diversification

There are some trading advisors who do not diversify their positions among a wide variety of commodities. In general, the more diversified the more conservative in the approach.

The grouping of related commodities that usually act in concert is a favored method used by trading advisors to diversify their futures positions. For example, there is the grain group, including wheat, corn, and oats; the soybean complex, which involves soybeans, soybean meal, and oil; metals; and foreign currencies. In some cases, the prices of commodities comprising these groups will be positively correlated; that is, their prices will move more or less in unison, up or down. On the other hand, among currencies, the U.S. dollar often correlates negatively with the major European currencies such as the West German mark and the Swiss franc. At various times, depending on prevailing or projected price and commodity trends, an advisor will manage portfolio risk through the diversification of futures positions both within and between different commodity groups, thus attempting to take advantage of historical price patterns in order to control volatility and increase return.

Trading Philosophies: Trend Following and Specialized Approaches

Different trading advisors approach the futures markets from a variety of perspectives. But recently advisors have fallen into two broad categories: trend followers and those who prefer a more specialized approach.

Trend Followers

In recent years the majority of successful trading advisors have been trend followers. Trend followers attempt to identify existing or emerging trends—characterized by sustained price movement, up or down—and then take positions in these trending markets. Because of unanticipated inflation, deflationary prices, wars, famine, weather conditions, government regulations, and the strength of the dollar, the "trending nature" of many of the commodity futures previously discussed has been sustained enough to result in the generation of attractive profits in managed accounts using trend following systems.

Technical and Fundamental Approaches

Trend followers use either technical analysis or fundamental analysis for determining market trends. Most successful trend followers use a wide variety of technical tools to help them identify trends and to judge the relative strength of a market trend. Computer trading models have been developed for these purposes, and can integrate moving averages, oscillators, relative strength indicators, and other technical tools for a variety of commodities.

The combination of technical analysis, which projects price movement based on historical data, and trend following has been very successful in recent years. Jesse H.

Thompson in his article "Trend Again?" (*Technical Analysis of Stocks & Commodities*, December 1984) studied recent industry surveys which show that of 14 top performing advisors over the past two to three years, 13 followed technical analysis and *all* of these 13 were *trend followers*.

Trend followers may also pay close attention to other, nontechnical factors, including seasonal commodity shifts, interest rate fluctuations, international trade and currency conditions, and government crop and related economic reports in varying degrees. However, the true trend follower will focus on emerging and strengthening market trends, to the exclusion of other conditions considered to be already reflected in the prices of the commodities.

There are, however, some trading advisors who rely primarily on fundamental analysis. These advisors project price movements according to conditions of supply and demand, such as the regulatory environment and market conditions, that would influence the price activity of a commodity. For example, an advisor involved with livestock futures would take into account such diverse but interrelated factors as current and projected livestock populations, the condition of grain feed crops, weather conditions, and related considerations. Also included is an ongoing scrutiny of the relationships existing at any given time between the price of the futures and the price of the actual commodity.

For most trading advisors managing larger, more diversified portfolios, fundamental analysis is impractical. Tracking the many commodities that make up a diversified futures account portfolio (16–22 positions) would require far too much time—a serious liability in the fast-paced futures market. For this reason, many advisors consider an approach based chiefly on fundamentals to be cumbersome and ultimately disadvantageous. However, many advisors today take certain key fundamental analyses and reports into account when judging the longer term strength, duration, or direction of a market trend.

Apart from the difficulty of tracking fundamentals on many commodities simultaneously, trading advisors relying on fundamental analysis alone are generally hampered by two other handicaps: they often move out of major trends too soon, thereby limiting profits on the upside; and, because they may follow fewer commodities, are limited in how broadly they can diversify—as a result portfolio risk is significantly increased.

Specialized Trading Approaches

There are other more specialized approaches utilized by some managers. It is our opinion that most of these approaches are too speculative for the investor who is not a full-time professional in the business. Some make greater use of different trading strategies such as spreads and straddles, in which one might buy or sell futures contracts in the same commodity but for different months simultaneously. Arbitrage, a more complex strategy employed principally in interest rate, currency, and stock index futures trading, involves taking advantage of short-term price differences that exist between the futures and cash markets.

Other trading advisors may specialize in the financial futures markets, offering programs geared to interest rate futures, currencies, options on financial futures, or futures on major stock market indexes such as the futures contract traded at the Chicago Mercantile Exchange on the Standard and Poor's 500 Stock Index. Such stock index futures provide a highly leveraged way for investors to profit from movements of the stock market without selecting individual stocks and without the expenses inherent in buying or selling significant amounts of stock.

Still other trading advisors, many of whom have come up as exchange floor traders or brokers, utilize a more speculative approach known as day trading. This approach involves the buying and selling of contracts, and liquidating all open positions within the same trading day. The goal is to profit quickly from short-term price fluctuations, as opposed to tracking major trends over extended periods of time. Generally, the conservative investor seeking limited downside risk and good returns from his futures account will not be as comfortable with such a short-term approach.

Day trading is also usually more costly because of frequent trading, resulting in higher commissions. It is also far more speculative. The vagaries of the marketplace on any particular day can themselves cause significant fluctuations in the prices of different commodity futures contracts. These fluctuations are taken into account by a trend follower. Over the course of a major trend, day-to-day fluctuations will occur, but the determining factor in the performance of the overall positions will be the longer-term trend and not the day-to-day fluctuations. Attempting to guess day-to-day changes can be a highly speculative undertaking, one which very few professionals are successful in pursuing.

Actual Trading Advisor Profiles

Although each individual trading advisor will have his or her own unique characteristics and background, there are enough similarities to make some general comments.

The typical trading advisor is a college educated specialist, often with a graduate degree in a scientific or technical area. In many cases, the advisor also has a mathematics and computer background and several years hands-on experience in the futures markets. Trading advisors today usually are between 40–50 years of age and, while they operate independently, they tend to have an operations and support staff as well as in-depth communications links to futures exchanges via clearing members throughout the country. A trading advisor need not be located at an exchange or even in a city with an exchange. Today's successful trading advisors are located throughout the country.

Let's take a brief look at the actual profiles of some of today's leading futures trading advisors:

Manager A: Undergraduate degree in accounting; former commodity broker; developed his own computer trading system in 1968, trading his own money with this system since 1971; seven years experience as a trading advisor for others.

Manager B: Undergraduate degree in engineering; M.B.A. from Harvard; former commodity broker and analyst; eight years as a trading advisor managing futures accounts.

Manager C: Undergraduate degree in chemical engineering and economics, and Masters degree in mechanical engineering; former securities analyst; 16 years as head of a computerized information system firm; seven years as a trading advisor.

Manager D: Undergraduate degree in engineering physics; doctorate degree in theoretical physics; 14 years experience in commodities markets; 10 years as analyst and manager of futures portfolios.

> **Manager E**: Undergraduate degree in business administration; certified public accountant; active futures trader for 30 years; seven years as manager and trading advisor.

These thumbnail sketches demonstrate the kinds of backgrounds of some of the more successful futures money managers. A broker should be able to provide a Disclosure Document and detailed personal histories of any prospective trading advisor to interested investors.

What to Look For When Selecting a Trading Advisor

What investors must look for are the trading advisors who best suit their particular investment goals and preferences regarding risk management and return on invested capital.

The authors suggest that investors pay close attention to the down periods, their frequency and duration, when examining a trading advisor's performance record. This is the most valid method of judging investor/advisor compatability. Some investors will prefer an advisor who can consistently show a conservative, risk-averse approach with an average 20–25 percent annual rate of return. Others will feel comfortable with a higher degree of risk in return for higher potential rewards.

In general look for the following nine characteristics when selecting a trading advisor:

In business successfully for three to ten years.

Has $3 million–$15 million under management.

Practices strict money and position management with high reserve levels and diversified accounts of 15 to 25 commodities traded in the portfolio.

Never overcommitted in one position; usually 2–8 percent of portfolio at risk per position.

Maximum downside "paper" risk of 20–30 percent for any calendar quarter with average annual rates of return of 30 percent for three or more years.

Provides full disclosure of actual results; does not use hypothetical or simulated results or models.

Allows a portion of reserves to be placed in interest-bearing accounts, usually U.S. Treasury bills.

Has fees and incentive arrangements that are competitive with industry standards.

Has no reported legal or compliance problems.

Finally, the risk/reward parameters can be customized to the individual investor through the use of a managed futures account. The better the individual investor understands his or her own risk/reward profile, the better the chance that an advisor will be found who represents that individual's investment outlook.

Chapter

7

Personalized Trading Approaches: Four Actual Accounts

How money is invested in a managed futures account.
How actual accounts look.

A portion of the equity that is put up by an investor to establish a managed futures account will be used by the trading advisor to fulfill margin requirements for futures positions. The allocation of the total sum invested in the account will depend greatly upon the trading advisor's approach to portfolio management. In Chapter 6, we defined the three principal portfolio management approaches—conservative, aggressive, and middle-of-the-road—each with its own unique combination of risk/reward characteristics with respect to account cash management and market participation.

We can begin to understand more clearly how accounts are managed in various ways that suit the needs of different investors by examining sample daily account statements (referred to as equity runs), generated from the actual trading activity of several accounts managed by different trading advisors. Equity runs provide an exemplary management tool because they indicate the value of the account and existing positions held in it at the close of *each* trading day.

Four Actual Accounts

In this chapter we examine four accounts with four different trading advisors. For reference purposes, the four accounts are identified as Customer Equity and Margin Status Reports A, B, C, and D.

A Conservative Account

In Example A (see pp. 88–89), the date of the equity run (7/19) is shown at the top. Additional information categories are identified by the column heads across the top of the chart, reading Trade Date; Position (long/short); Option and Commodity (with contract months); Trade Price; and Equity (debit/credit).

The **trade date** refers to the date at which the trade was first executed to open the position. All of the indicated trades refer to contract positions held in the account at the close of trading on the date indicated at the top of the equity run sheet.

Positions held in the account can be **long** (futures contracts bought expecting prices to rise) or **short** (contracts sold expecting prices to decline). These trades are existing positions called open trades. After adding debits and credits, the resulting value is called the **total open trade equity**—in other words, the value of all open (not closed out) positions in the account.

The number of contracts bought or sold is indicated in the **position** column, with the number of contracts long or short indicated as shown in the example.

The type of contract is indicated in the column headed **option & commodity (contract months)**, and the price at which the trade was executed is noted with the commodity name and also in the trade price column as the first price entry. The price shown directly below in the trade price column for that commodity is the closing price for that day.

Finally, the current profit or loss status of each position is indicated in the **equity debit** or **credit** column. This represents the profit or loss for each open trade position.

Toward the bottom of the sheet, the total open trade equity and total equity are indicated, along with a dollar amount for the value of any securities, such as Treasury bills, held in the account. Adding the **beginning account balance** (first variable line under heading, A/C Bal.) and **total open trade equity** gives the **total equity**. Adding the **total equity** figure and the **securities on deposit** total gives the **total net asset value** of the account, less any fees and commissions due, at the close of trading for a particular day.

In Example A, the position established on 6/05 by going short one September cocoa futures contract shows a profit of $4,180. Similarly, the position established on 6/19 by going long two August cattle futures contracts shows a profit, exactly one month later, of $400.

By looking at the number of positions held in different commodity markets, the number of contracts in these positions, we can determine how aggressively or conservatively the trading advisor is trading the account.

For example, trading advisor A is moderately conservative in his approach as we can see from the fact that the portfolio is well rounded and highly diversified among a variety of commodities. There are 22 commodities with open trades in the portfolio. Of the 22 commodities, the trading advisor is long in only two commodities—T-bill futures and cattle futures—and short in 20 markets. This tells us that the trader expects a broad bear market in most commodities, an assessment we can see is correct when we observe that the account shows only credits (profits) and no losses for all the open trades held in the account.

The trading advisor is disciplined in that he lets those positions with profits run, while quickly closing out positions that show losses. In addition, most of the positions include a small number of contracts, usually only one or two, except in the case of grains, where single contract sizes are generally indicated by a "5," signifying 5,000 bushels or one standard size contract. Trading this size contract also indicates a generally conservative approach.

Another indication of the conservative nature of the account and its trading advisor is shown in the relationship between margin deposits and net asset value. In this case margin deposits are between 20–25 percent of the account's net asset value.

In general, we can say that trading advisor A is conservative in his overall approach, and that for this particular date (7/19) his strategy is to participate in a broad deflationary commodity price trend.

An Aggressive Account

Example B (see p. 90) illustrates another account with a different trading advisor. The account shows much less commodity diversification than Example A, with only 13 commodities showing open trade positions. In addition, the number of contracts long (purchased) and short (sold) is higher than in the previous example. On the other hand, this trading advisor also tends to let profits run, as shown by the fact that eight positions show a profit while only five indicate a loss, and that the average winning (credit) position is three times greater than the average losing (debit) position. Comparing Example B to Example A, we can establish that trading advisor B is more willing to assume risk in search of higher percentage returns, and that B is the more aggressive of the two advisors.

A Middle-of-the-Road Account

Example C (see pp. 91–92) shows a highly diversified portfolio, similar to Example A, with 19 commodities showing open trade positions as of 1/18. Open trade positions are more evenly distributed between long and short positions (8 and 11) than in the case of Example A. Losses are indicated in only four commodities, and these losses are relatively small. The relationship between margin deposits and net asset value approximates 30–35 percent, a slightly more aggressive approach than in the conservative account shown in Example A above.

Based on this information, we assume that trading advisor C is generally conservative in overall approach, but somewhat less conservative than advisor A, with respect to market participation. In terms of performance and philosophy, trading advisor C represents a typical middle-of-the-road approach in managed account trading.

An Ultra-Conservative Account

The final example, D (see pp. 93–94), is dated 7/19, the same date as in Example A. Example D is somewhat less diversified and shows very small positions in terms of the number of contracts held in open trades. All of the positions except one (hogs) are composed of only one contract; and with the single exception of the one long Treasury bond future, all the positions are short. The only loss that appears here is in the T-bond future, with all other open trades showing a profit.

Trading advisor D is clearly the most conservative of the

four advisors. He has let his profits run as he successfully-
hedges a broad deflationary commodity trend, and he is
very quick to close out losing positions in order to cut his
losses. Overall, D is an excellent example of a very conservative approach to trading a managed futures account.

As this examination of equity runs demonstrates, the performance of various trading advisors is essential to investors
who seek an advisor whose approach—and results—conform
to their individual comfort levels.

Customer Equity & Margin Status Report—Example A: A Conservative Approach

| TRADE DATE | POSITION | | OPTION & COMMODITY | TRADE PRICE | EQUITY | |
	LONG	SHORT			DEBIT	CREDIT
			A/C BAL.–REG.			3,017.50
07-19-XX						
06-14-XX		10	SEPT XX WHEAT	3.58 3/4		1,225.00
	*	10 *	3.587 AVG	3.46 1/2		1,225.00 *
07-06-XX		5	SEP XX CORN	3.13		87.50
	*	5 *	3.130 AVG	3.11 1/4		87.50 *
06-26-XX		10	AUG XX SOYBEANS	7.72		8,100.00
	*	10 *	7.720 AVG	6.91		8,100.00 *
06-26-XX		1	SEPT XX BEAN OIL	32.10		2,340.00
	*	1 *	32.100 AVG	28.20		2,340.00 *
06-12-XX		3	DEC XX 1000 SILV	920.00		4,290.00
	*	3 *	920.000 AVG	777.00		4,290.00 *
06-13-XX		2	AUG XX KILO GOLD	380.50		2,025.46
	*	2 *	380.500 AVG	349.00		2,025.46 *
06-05-XX		1	SEPT XX NEW COCOA	25.66		4,180.00
	*	1 *	25.660 AVG	21.48		4,180.00 *
06-13-XX		2	OCT XX SUGAR II	6.08		3,203.20
	*	2 *	6.080 AVG	4.65		3,203.20 *
06-13-XX		1	SEP XX COFFEE C	145.25		1,638.75
	*	1 *	145.250 AVG	140.88		1,638.75 *

Customer Equity & Margin Status Report—Example A:
A Conservative Approach, *Concluded*

TRADE DATE	POSITION LONG	POSITION SHORT	OPTION & COMMODITY	TRADE PRICE	EQUITY DEBIT	EQUITY CREDIT
06-05-XX		2	DEC XX COTTON	75.11		6,340.00
	*	2 *	75.110 AVG	68.77		6,340.00 *
06-12-XX		1	SEP XX B–POUND	139.35		1,700.00
	*	1 *	139.350 AVG	132.55		1,700.00 *
06-08-XX		1	SEP XX C–DOLLAR	76.870		1,720.00
	*	1 *	76.870 AVG	75.150		1,720.00 *
06-19-XX		1	SEP XX D–MARK	36.660		1,512.50
	*	1 *	366.600 AVG	35.450		1,512.50 *
06-15-XX		2	SEP XX S–FRANCS	44.700		6,900.00
	*	2 *	447.000 AVG	41.940		6,900.00 *
06-08-XX		1	SEP XX J–YEN	43.820		2,950.00
	*	1 *	438.200 AVG	41.460		2,950.00 *
06-15-XX	2		SEP XX T–BILLS	89.33		550.00
	2 *	*	89.330 AVG	89.44		550.00 *
06-26-XX		1	SEP XX COPPER	60.50		25.00
	*	1 *	60.500 AVG	60.40		25.00 *
06-19-XX	2		AUG XX CATTLE	63.90		400.00
	2 *	*	63.900 AVG	64.40		400.00 *
06-29-XX		1	AUG XX PK BELLY	61.65		2,717.00
	*	1 *	61.650 AVG	54.50		2,717.00 *
06-25-XX		1	SEP XX LUMBER	139.10		2,288.00
	*	1 *	139.100 AVG	121.50		2,288.00 *
06-27-XX		4	SEP XX MINI–VALUE	173.70		2,220.00
	*	4 ⁹	173.700 AVG	168.15		2,220.00 *
07-10-XX		2	SEP XX HEAT OIL	77.30		1,024.80
	*	2 *	77.300 AVG	76.08		1,024.80 *
**********	"0" ****				TOT OT EQ	57,437.21**
*	44,200	I M	.00 LOV .00 WF		TOT EQ	60,454.71
*	27,864	MM	.00 SOV 16254.71 ME			
08-30-XX			NO. 00001 US T–BILL	128,583.72		
			SECURITIES ON DEP. TOTAL	128,583.72 *		
			TOTAL VALUE OF ACCOUNT			189,038.43

Customer Equity & Margin Status Report—Example B:
A More Aggressive Approach

TRADE DATE	POSITION LONG	POSITION SHORT	OPTION & COMMODITY	TRADE PRICE	EQUITY DEBIT	EQUITY CREDIT
			A/C BAL.–REG.			26,936.28
04-25-XX						
03-23-XX	15		MAY XX CORN	3.10		600.00
	15 *	*	3.100 AVG	3.14		600.00 *
03-23-XX	15		JUL XX SOYBEANS	6.45		2,437.50
	15 *	*	6.450 AVG	6.61 1/4		2,437.50 *
03-23-XX	5		JUL XX BEAN MEAL	193.00		400.00
	5 *	*	193.000 AVG	193.80		400.00 *
04-19-XX	7		OCT XX SUGAR II	8.50		2,508.80
	7 *	*	8.500 AVG	8.82		2,508.80 *
04-22-XX	3		JUL XX COFFEE C	125.40	90.00	
	3 *	*	125.400 AVG	125.32	90.00 *	
04-18-XX	3		JUN XX B–POUND	155.45		825.00
	3 *	*	155.450 AVG	156.55		825.00 *
03-23-XX		1	JUN XX S–FRANCS	48.550	512.50	
	*	1 *	485.500 AVG	48.960	512.50 *	
03-20-XX	2		JUN XX CATTLE	68.60	1,040.00	
	2 *	*	68.600 AVG	67.30	1,040.00 *	
04-11-XX		2	JUL XX HOGS	53.22 1/2		1,650.00
	*	2 *	53.225 AVG	60.47 1/2		1,650.00 *
03-24-XX		1	MAY XX PK BELLY	71.35		731.50
	*	1 *	71.350 AVG	69.42 1/2		731.50 *
04-20-XX		3	AUG XX FEEDERS	65.10	297.00	
	*	3 *	65.100 AVG	65.32 1/2	297.00 *	
03-23-XX	1		JUN XX KC VAL LN	178.80		4,625.00
	1 *	*	178.800 AVG	188.05		4,625.00 *
04-19-XX	3		JUL XX HEAT OIL	80.40	1,058.40	
	3 *	*	80.400 AVG	79.56	1,058.40 *	
**********	"0" ****				TOT OT EQ	10,779.90**
*	56,250	I M	.00 LOV .00 WF		TOT EQ	37,716.18
*	36,741	MM	.00 SOV .00 ME			
07-14-XX			NO. 00001 US T–BILL	48,971.19		
			SECURITIES ON DEP. TOTAL	48,971.19 *		
			TOTAL VALUE OF ACCOUNT			86,687.37

Customer Equity & Margin Status Report—Example C:
A Middle-of-the Road Approach

TRADE DATE	POSITION LONG	POSITION SHORT	OPTION & COMMODITY	TRADE PRICE	EQUITY DEBIT	EQUITY CREDIT
			A/C BAL.–REG.			48,214.58
01-18-XX						
01-17-XX		10	MAR XX WHEAT	3.54		550.00
	*	10 *	3.540 AVG	3.48 1/2		550.00 *
01-03-XX		10	MAR XX CORN	3.31		250.00
	*	10 *	3.310 AVG	3.28 1/2		250.00 *
01-09-XX		5	MAR XX SOYBEANS	7.76		1,825.00
	*	5 *	7.760 AVG	7.39 1/2		1,825.00 *
01-04-XX	1		MAR XX GNMA	68 28/32		875.00
	1 *	*	68.875 AVG	69 24/32		875.00 *
01-16-XX	1		MAR XX T–BONDS	71 20/32	343.75	
	1 *	*	71.628 AVG	71 9/32	343.75 *	
11-21-XX		1	MAR XX SUGAR II	9.98		2,441.60
	*	1 *	9.980 AVG	7.80		2,441.60 *
01-04-XX		1	MAR XX COFFEE C	137.25	1,773.75	
	*	1 *	137.250 AVG	141.98	1,773.75 *	
12-20-XX		1	MAR XX COTTON	78.33		1,245.00
	*	1 *	78.330 AVG	75.84		1,245.00 *
01-04-XX		3	MAR XX B–POUND	141.80		375.00
	*	3 *	141.800 AVG	141.30		375.00 *
01-04-XX		2	MAR XX D–MARK	36.170		600.00
	*	2 *	361.700 AVG	35.930		600.00 *
12-28-XX	2		MAR XX J–YEN	43.200	425.00	
	2 *	*	432.000 AVG	43.030	425.00 *	
01-03-XX	2		MAR XX T–BILLS	90.86		650.00
	2 *	*	90.860 AVG	90.99		650.00 *
12-16-XX		1	FEB XX GOLD–COMX	385.00		1,480.00
	*	1 *	385.000 AVG	370.20		1,480.00 *
01-12-XX	2		APR XX CATTLE	68.85		680.00
	2 *	*	68.850 AVG	69.57 1/2		680.00 *
01-12-XX	2		APR XX HOGS	49.60		555.00
	2 *	*	49.600 AVG	50.62 1/2		555.00 *
11-18-XX	2		MAR XX FEEDERS	66.50		4,466.00
	2 *	*	66.500 AVG	71.57 1/2		4,466.00 *

Customer Equity & Margin Status Report—Example C:
A Middle-of-the Road Approach, *Concluded*

TRADE DATE	POSITION		OPTION & COMMODITY	TRADE PRICE	EQUITY	
	LONG	SHORT			DEBIT	CREDIT
12-13-XX		1	MAR XX LUMBER	158.30		2,093.00
	*	1 *	183.300 AVG	172.20		2,093.00 *
01-16-XX	1		APR XX HEAT OIL	77.80	117.60	
	1 *	*	77.800 AVG	77.52	117.60 *	
12-15-XX		1	APR XX PLATINUM	398.00		1,055.00
	*	1 *	398.000 AVG	376.90		1,055.00 *
**********	"0" ****				TOT OT EQ	16,380.50**
*	37,250	I M	.00 LOV .00 WF		TOT EQ	64,595.08
*	26,400	MM	.00 SOV 27346.08 ME			
03-01-XX			NO. 00001 US T–BILL	49,323.33		
			SECURITIES ON DEP. TOTAL	49,323.33 *		
			TOTAL VALUE OF ACCOUNT			113,918.41

Customer Equity & Margin Status Report—Example D:
An Ultra-Conservative Approach

TRADE DATE	POSITION LONG	POSITION SHORT	OPTION & COMMODITY	TRADE PRICE	EQUITY DEBIT	EQUITY CREDIT
			A/C BAL.–REG.			38,237.87
07-19-XX						
07-06-XX		5	DEC XX WHEAT	3.65 1/4		187.50
	*	5 *	3.652 AVG	3.61 1/2		187.50 *
07-06-XX		5	NOV XX SOYBEANS	6.61		1,050.00
	*	5 *	6.610 AVG	6.40		1,050.00 *
07-13-XX	1		DEC XX T–BONDS	62 15/32	156.25	
	1 *	*	62.468 AVG	62 10/32	156.25 *	
06-11-XX		1	SEP XX NEW COCOA	24.15		2,670.00
	*	1 *	24.150 AVG	21.48		2,670.00 *
06-20-XX		1	SEP XX COFFEE C	140.90		7.50
	*	1 *	140.900 AVG	140.88		7.50 *
06-15-XX		1	OCT XX COTTON	74.65		2,975.00
	*	1 *	74.650 AVG	68.70		2,975.00 *
06-13-XX		1	SEP XX S–FRANCS	44.900		3,700.00
	*	1 *	449.000 AVG	41.940		3,700.00 *
05-11-XX		1	SEP XX J–YEN	44.260		3,500.00
	*	1 *	442.600 AVG	41.460		3,500.00 *
05-22-XX		1	SEP XX S&P INDEX	157.30		2,650.00
	*	1 *	157.300 AVG	152.00		2,650.00 *
06-21-XX		1	DEC XX COPPER	63.25		275.00
	*	1 *	63.250 AVG	62.15		275.00 *
04-06-XX		1	AUG XX GOLD–COMX	393.80		4,550.00
	*	1 *	393.800 AVG	348.30		4,550.00 *
05-29-XX		2	AUG XX HOGS	56.95		1,740.00
	*	2 *	56.950 AVG	54.05		1,740.00 *
07-11-XX		1	NOV XX LUMBER	136.20		949.00
	*	1 *	136.200 AVG	128.90		949.00 *
06-15-XX		1	SEP XX HEAT OIL	79.05		1,247.40
	*	1 *	79.050 AVG	76.08		1,247.40 *

Customer Equity & Margin Status Report—Example D:
An Ultra-Conservative Approach, *Concluded*

TRADE DATE	POSITION		OPTION & COMMODITY	TRADE PRICE	EQUITY	
	LONG	SHORT			DEBIT	CREDIT
**********	"0" *****				TOT OT EQ	25,345.15**
*	25,950	I M	.00 LOV .00 WF		TOT EQ	63,583.02
	16,901	MM	.00 SOV 37633.02 ME			
08-30-XX			NO. 00001 US T-BILL	54,432.34		
			SECURITIES ON DEP. TOTAL	54,432.34 *		
			TOTAL VALUE OF ACCOUNT			118,015.36

Chapter 8

What Are the Costs?
Fees, Brokerage and
Tax Considerations

What you can expect to pay for the management of your account:
Commissions, fees, and taxes.
Actual examples of cost calculations.

As with any investment advisory service or money management approach, a managed futures account program has costs associated with it. These costs fall into three major categories:

1. Money management fees:
   a. Performance or incentive.
   b. Management or administrative.
2. Brokerage commissions.
3. Taxes.

We will review each of these investment costs and then show how they are computed with sample calculations and illustrations.

Investment Costs

Money Management Fees

A *performance fee* is based on the results produced by the advisor for the account. In general, the performance fee is

15 percent of the net new profits in the account, calculated and paid on a quarterly basis. This means that the advisor has to make up any losses before the investor can be charged a further performance fee.

In most cases, the trading advisor receives a *management fee* of 1.5 percent per quarter. For investors who may be more familiar with stock accounts, this percentage may appear high. However, futures are leveraged instruments, so that your investment can actually control an average of five times the amount of equity as in a similar size stock account. Therefore, futures management fees when compared on a dollars under management basis are, in fact, quite comparable to those of equity accounts. This fee is based on the current net asset value of the account.

In addition, a further advantage of commodity investing is that part of the account's funds can be held in the form of short-term Treasury bills. The investor usually receives the interest on the T-bills (technically the discount paid at maturity). As federal securities, the T-bills can be used as a margin deposit, and the interest earned can be considered as income to offset commission and/or money management fees. Income earned from Treasury bills is taxed as ordinary income.

Brokerage Commission

The brokerage firm through which the managed account is cleared receives commissions on all executed trades. However, the trading advisor has sole authority to trade the account, and *it is important to note that it is in the interest of the advisor to keep the number of commissionable trades to a minimum*, as commissions reduce profits and lower the net asset value of the account, which serves to reduce the incentive and administrative fees earned. In addition, they adversely affect the advisor's public performance record.

Unlike securities brokerage commissions, which are charged for both the sale and/or purchase of securities, commissions on futures are charged only upon closing out a position. This is referred to as a *round turn*, and commissions are charged per round turn.

Futures commissions can vary by commodity traded, or be charged at a flat rate, regardless of the commodity traded. Rates for a managed account range from $60 to as much as $120 per round turn. The industry average will fall in the $80 to $100 range. Commissions charged by discount brokers for self-managed accounts tend to be much lower, but do not offer the management, expertise, and safeguards of a professionally managed account program.

For the vast majority of commodity transactions, commissions amount to far less than for a securities account of equal value. Take, for example, a contract for pork bellies worth $26,000 (70¢ × 38,000 lbs.). Compare a $70 round turn commission for this futures contract to the commission probably charged for securities of equal value. Now, assume a purchase and sale of 1,000 shares of stock at $26 per share. For the commission costs to be equal, the investor would have to be charged only three and a half cents per share of stock, far less than what even discount stock brokers could charge, and certainly far less than even institutional rates.

Over one year, the overall commission rate for a managed futures account is likely to be between 10 and 20 percent of your equity, averaging 15 percent—far less than the 40 to 60 percent often experienced when an individual account executive works directly with a client in a self-directed rather than a managed futures account.

Taxes

The Tax Reform Act of 1984, section 1256, states that commodity futures contracts are taxed on the basis of a 60/40 formula. That is, gains and losses from both open and closed contracts are treated as 60 percent long-term capital gain or loss, and 40 percent short-term capital gain or loss. Contracts are taxed on a marked-to-market basis; that is, all profits and losses must be declared on all contracts—opened and closed—on the last trading day of the taxable year.

Under the 60/40 rule, gains are subject to a maximum tax rate that equals 32 percent, assuming the tax payer has an effective tax rate of 50 percent.

Futures are one of the few investments where long-term capital gain is available *for periods of less than six months.* And they are the *only* investment that permits short positions to be closed out with a long-term capital gain.

This rule applies to all commodities futures contracts, currency futures contracts, stock-index futures contracts, options on futures, and exchange-listed stock options.

Actual Examples of Cost Calculations

Let's look at some examples of how to calculate account value, management and performance fees, and federal taxes for a managed futures account.

Calculating Account Value

Table 8–1 provides an example of an account with an original account size of $50,000. Item 1 indicates that the account balance at the beginning of the period was $25,000. This represents the cash in the account from a previous reporting period that was either not yet invested or the result of closed-out account activity from a prior period.

The trading results from closed-out trades show profits of $4,500 and losses of $1,500, or a net trading profit of

Table 8–1
Calculating Account Value

1. Beginning Account Balance		$25,000.	

2. Closed–out trades

	Profits =	$ 4,500.		
	Losses =	1,500.		
		$ 3,000.	+ 3,000.	
				$28,000.

3. Commissions
(four closed–out trades at $75. each)   −   300.
                                                                      $27,700.

4. Open Trades (Market–to–Market)

	Credits =	$12,000.		
	Debits =	5,000.		
		$ 7,000.	+ 7,000.	
				$34,700.

5. Securities on Deposit   = $24.800.   +24,800.
   ($25,000 at maturity)

NET ASSET VALUE	$59,500.	*
ORIGINAL ACCOUNT SIZE	$50,000.	
PROFIT	$ 9,500.	**

*   used to calculate administrative fee
**   used to calculate incentive fee

$3,000. This $3,000 is added to the beginning balance of $25,000, yielding a sum of $28,000. Commissions totalling $300 are deducted, leaving a balance of $27,700. Open-trade positions show credits totalling $12,000, and debits totalling $5,000, for an open-trade credit of $7,000. This gives us a new balance of $34,700. Item 5 indicates that a portion of the account is held in short-term Treasury bills. If we add the value of the T-bills held in the account, $24,800, we arrive at a new net asset value of the account of $59,500. Thus, the account shows a profit of $9,500. This net profit is used to calculate the advisor's performance or incentive fee. The net asset value is used to calculate the administrative or management fee.

Let's track this sample account through an entire year (see Table 8–2), assuming that the data in Table 8–1 describe first quarter results for the year.

Calculating Money Management Fees and Pre-Tax Profits

The original equity for this account was $50,000, and first quarter results produces a net asset value of $59,500 ($50,000 initial equity plus $9,500 profits). To calculate the management fee for the first quarter, multiply $59,500 by 1.5 percent to obtain $892.50. Deduct this management fee from the net asset value to arrive at the account's net new profits of $8,607.50. The quarterly incentive fee (15 percent of net new profits) is $1,291.13.

In the second quarter, the account grew to $65,000, with management fees of $975 and an incentive fee of $812.63 for the second quarter.

In the third quarter, assume that the net asset value of the account temporarily retraces to $60,000. The quarterly management fee is $900, but, because there are no new profits in the quarter, there is no performance fee.

The following table summarizes the method by which management fees and pre-tax profits are calculated.

Table 8–2
Calculating Money Management Fees and Pre-Tax Profit
(By Quarters)

Original Equity = $50,000.00

	First	Second	Third	Fourth
Ending N.A.V. (net asset value)	$59,500.00	$65,000.00	$60,000.00	$75,000.00
Management Fee	× 0.015	× 0.015	× 0.015	× 0.015
(1.5% per quarter)	$ 892.50	$ 975.00	$ 900.00	$ 1,125.00
* N.A.V. less management fee	$58,607.50	$64,025.00	$59,100.00	$73,875.00
Net New Profits	$ 8,607.50	$ 5,417.50	($ 4,925.00)	$ 9,850.00
Incentive Fee				
(15% of new net profits)	× 0.15	× 0.15	—	× 0.15
	$ 1,291.13	$ 812.63	—	$ 1,477.50

* Highest value is point at which net new profits are established.
   (In this example, for the first through third quarters, that value is $64,025.00)

Summary and Pre-Tax Profit

Original Equity	= $50,000.00	Management Fees	=	$ 3,892.50
Equity Gain	= 25,000.00	Incentive Fees	=	3,581.26
		Total Fees	=	7,473.76
		Pre–Tax Profit	=	17,526.24
				35%

Note: Commissions have already been deducted when calculating the Net Asset Value of the Account.

Finally, in the fourth quarter, the account appreciates to $75,000. The management fee is $1,125, and the performance fee, based on net new profits of $9,850, is $1,477.50.

As we can see in the year's summary, the sample account here has grown from $50,000 to $75,000, for an annual equity gain of $25,000. The total management and incentive fees for the year came to $7,473.76 for a total pretax profit of $17,526.24 after deducting all fees and commissions, or a 35 percent rate of return.

Calculating (Maximum) Federal Taxes

Finally, let's calculate the federal tax on this same account. Table 8–3, Example 1, shows that 60 percent of gains or losses are considered long-term and 40 percent are considered short-term. For an account with a total gain of $100,000 the total tax paid is $32,000, or 32 percent.

For our sample account, look at Table 8–3, Example 2. The total gain was $17,562.24 before taxes. After deducting for capital gains at 60 percent and assuming the taxpayer is in the 50 percent bracket, total taxes paid come to $5,608.40. For this account, then, total profits—after all fees, commissions, and federal taxes—are $11,953.84 for an effective after-tax return of 23.8 percent.

Table 8–3
Calculating Maximum Federal Tax

Example 1
For a Tax Payer in 50% Bracket

Total Gain	Portion Considered Long Term (60%)	Portion Considered Short Term (40%)
$100,000	$60,000	$40,000
Less capital gain deduction at 60%	–36,000	
Portion taxed at regular rates	24,000 +	40,000
	$64,000 x 50%	
Maximum Total Tax	$32,000 (32%)	

Example 2
For Our Prior Example, Table 8–2

Total Gain	Portion Considered Long Term (60%)	Portion Considered Short Term (40%)
$17,562.24	$10,515.74	$7,010.50
Less capital gain deduction at 60%	– 6,309.44	
Portion taxed at regular rates	4,206.30 +	7,010.50
	$11,216.80 x 50%	
Total Tax	$ 5,608.40 (32%)	

After Tax Profitability

Beginning Account Size	=	$50,000.00
Annual Pre-tax Profit	=	17,562.24
MAXIMUM TAX (32%)	=	5,608.40
AFTER TAX PROFIT	=	11,953.84 (23.8%)

Chapter
9

Your Commitment to Success: Time and Money

How long should capital be committed to a managed account in order to achieve success?
What are the capital requirements?
Further increasing account diversification for reduced volatility.

Minimum Time Requirements

In return for the kind of professional portfolio management that an investor can obtain through a managed futures account, the investor should be willing to commit money for a certain amount of time because of the way commodity markets function.

Most experts agree that investors should consider an investment in a managed futures account in the same light as a real estate investment. Therefore, we suggest keeping at least the initial capital fully invested in the account for a period of one to three years. The fundamental reason for this time frame is to provide sufficient time for the emergence and full development of several cyclical major pricing trends in the commodities markets to take place. It is only through the effective management of the account during the evolution of such trends that significant profits can be made with a relatively high degree of assurance.

Experience has shown that most investors who have lost money in managed futures portfolios chose to close out those accounts prematurely, *usually after only four or five months.*

Above all else, the investor should be willing to ask the important question, "Do I view this futures account as a long-term investment or as a short-term speculative gamble?" If the answer indicates that the managed futures account is not being considered as an investment program, then chances are the investor will not be utilizing this instrument in the most effective way. It is a long-term, conservative investment approach which, like real estate, will be exposed to cyclical markets.

Minimum Capital Requirements

What is a reasonable initial investment in such an account? The answer depends largely on the total value of the investor's present portfolio. As a general rule, the individual with less than $50,000 to invest should *not* consider opening a managed account, but might consider a commodity pool or public commodity fund, where $2,000 to $5,000 minimums exist.

The minimum required by many trading advisors is an initial investment of $50,000 for a fully diversified individually managed account. It is our opinion that this amount is the minimum required to establish a conservatively managed account containing between six and ten commodity positions—the minimum we feel necessary for adequate diversification. An account with $100,000 would have between 15 and 22 positions, and in general we prefer this greater degree of diversification.

Increased Diversification for Reduced Volatility

For accounts with greater capitalization, the use of two different trading advisors with different systems can significantly reduce volatility through diversification. The strength of such a program is illustrated in Figure 9–1.

In Figure 9–1, the solid line represents the results over time of an account managed by trading advisor B. The dotted line represents the trading results of an account managed by trading advisor A. Both managers achieve continued profitability, but each shows wave-like characteristics of greater and lesser profitability. The objective is to establish

Figure 9–1
Reducing Portfolio Volatility

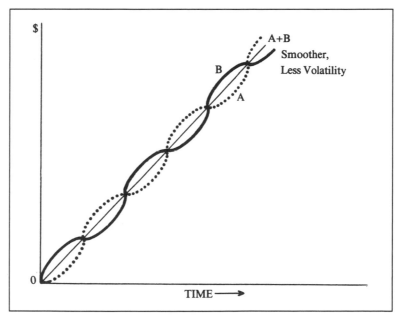

If managers A and B are both profitable, a portfolio of both managers will have a lower volatility than the individual managers.

Source: Fred S. Gehm, "Analyzing Risk/Reward Tradeoffs," *Technical Analysis of Stocks & Commodities*, March–April 1984.

accounts with trading advisors who not only trade prof-
itably but do so over periods of time in negative correlation.
That is, when manager A shows less profitability, manager
B, in the same period, shows greater profitability, and vice
versa. The straight diagonal line between the wavey lines
representing the trading advisors shows that the overall result will be to maintain a more constant profit with reduced
portfolio volatility.

An example of how this approach works can be seen in
Table 9–1 which shows how annual rates of return for two
trading advisors positively balance the performance of the
combined portfolio.

Table 9–1
Reducing Portfolio Volatility

Year	Manager 1	Manager 2	Average Return
1981	38%	28%	33%
1982	13	57	35
1983	38	(5)	16.5
1984	35	44	39.5
4 year average	31%	31%	31%

Chapter
10

The Mechanics of
Opening an Account

Understanding trading advisor forms and brokerage forms.
To whom do you make out the check?

As is the case with any professionally managed investment program, there are several legally required forms and statements which the investor will need to read, understand, and sign before a managed futures account can be established for trading. The entire process of opening an account takes less than an hour, and can be done in person or by discussion over the phone. This chapter summarizes the necessary documents and provides some examples for reference. (See Exhibits 10–1 through 10–9 at the end of the chapter.) These examples are included strictly for informational purposes, and are not intended for solicitation.

When opening a managed futures account, the investor should be aware that there are three principal parties involved in the ownership, management, and trading of the account: the investor, the broker-manager, and the trading advisor. It is the broker-manager who usually provides the forms and is responsible for the execution, reporting, and clearing of trades for the account.

The various documents and forms under discussion deal with the responsibilities of these three parties. They are standardized agreements designed to protect the investing public by the Commodity Futures Trading Commission (CFTC) and the National Futures Association (NFA), which together regulate the futures industry.

Trading Advisor Forms

The primary account document called the **Disclosure Document**, is required by the CFTC and is provided to the investor by the registered Commodity Trading Advisor (CTA). The Disclosure Document is similar to a securities prospectus. It contains the name and address of the trading advisor responsible for the management of the account, as well as a description of the advisor's trading practices, performance records, business background, fees, and a risk disclosure statement. This general Disclosure Document must be current, within the past six months, and include:

> An **advisory agreement** stating the size of the account and its basic conduct, to be signed by the trading advisor and the investor.

It may also contain:

> A **fee payment authorization** form authorizing the broker to pay the advisor's agreed upon fees from the account.

> A **disclosure document receipt** signed by the investor confirming receipt of the necessary disclosure materials.

Brokerage Forms

The investor will also receive several brokerage forms dealing with the opening of an account with the broker. These forms also require suitability information from the investor, as well as agreements stating the responsibilities of both broker and investor. These include:

A **client information form** requiring the name and address of the investor, along with references, tax identification or social security number, and an abbreviated financial statement. The broker will also provide the appropriate documents identifying the form of ownership of the account as an individual or sole proprietor, a joint account or partnership, or a trust or corporate account. This last account will also require a certificate of corporate resolution.

A **client agreement** form containing a standard contract with a futures commission merchant.

A **limited power of attorney** form authorizing the trading advisor to conduct futures trading on the account while disallowing any transfer or other use of the funds comprising the account.

A **trading advisor letter**, addressed to the relevant broker or futures commission merchant and signed by the investor informing the futures commission merchant of the investor's authorization for the payment of the advisor's fees and of the existence of the agreement between the investor and the designated trading advisor.

A CFTC **Risk Disclosure Statement**, required by the federal regulatory commission, informing the investor of the potential risks of commodity futures trading.

An **options disclosure statement** from the CFTC regulations describing the risks and uses of options on futures, such as gold, currency, or agricultural options, which can be used to hedge a variety of futures positions.

An **arbitration agreement** form (not always included) allowing the investor to pursue out-of-court settlement of any claims or disputes.

To Whom Do You Make Out Your Check?

For the client's protection, upon opening the account a check is made out to the *brokerage firm*—not the trading advisor—where it should be deposited in a customer-segregated account. In addition, one should only use a brokerage firm that is a *clearing member* of the major exchanges.

Exhibit 10–1
Trading Advisor Letter

In connection with my retention of the services of a commodity trading advisor, please be advised that C.S.A., Inc.'s Account Executive provided me with the names of the advisors on C.S.A., Inc.'s "Approved List". I reviewed the information and descriptions regarding advisors named on the list and decided to retain the services of _____.

I understand that you are not responsible for the trading decisions made by the advisor and I am aware that the trading advisor has published trading results which are available to me. I recognize that you have not undertaken to audit these results and that any stated results are not indicative of future performance.

I understand that you are not responsible for enforcing any equity restrictions described in the advisor's trading program, and that, although you intend to monitor the trading by the advisor of my account, you will not be responsible for ensuring that trading activity conforms to any model portfolio or other account description agreed to between me and the trading advisor. I hereby agree to hold you and your officers, directors, affiliates, and employees harmless from any and all liability arising out of a failure to observe the equity restrictions mentioned above, or to conform the trading in my account with any model portfolio or other account description agreed to between me and the trading advisor.

I hereby authorize you to remit all fees payable to _____ in accordance with our agreement dated _____. The above named trading advisor will present you with bills for fees as they become due and payable. I understand that you will not verify the accuracy of such bills and I authorize and instruct you to rely upon such fee computations as the trading advisor renders.

Very truly yours,

Date

_____

Signature of Client
(If More Than One, All Principals to the Account Must Sign)

x _____

x _____

x _____

x _____

Exhibit 10–2
Limited Power of Attorney
Authorization and Indemnity

a. Trading Authorization

The undersigned hereby authorizes _____ as his agent and attorney in fact (hereinafter referred to as "agent") to buy and sell (including short sales) securities, commodities, commodity futures contracts and or options on margin or otherwise for the undersigned's account and risk.

The undersigned hereby agrees to indemnify and hold you harmless from all loss, cost, indebtedness and liabilities arising therefrom.

In all such purchases and sales you are authorized to follow the instructions of the agent in every respect concerning the undersigned's account with you; except as herein otherwise provided, he is authorized to act for the undersigned in the same manner and with the same force and effect as the undersigned might or could do with respect to such purchases and sales as well as with respect to all other things necessary or incidental thereto, except that he is not authorized to withdraw any money, securities, or other property either in the name of the undersigned or otherwise.

The undersigned hereby ratifies and confirms any and all transactions with you heretofore or hereafter made by the agent on behalf of or for the account of the undersigned.

This authorization and indemnity is in addition to (and in no way limits or restricts) any rights which you may have under any other agreement between you and the undersigned.

This authorization and indemnity is a continuing one and shall remain in full force and effect until revoked by the undersigned by a written notice addressed to you and delivered to you at the office where the undersigned's account is carried, but such revocation shall not affect any liability in any way resulting from transactions initiated prior to such revocation. This authorization and indemnity shall inure to the benefit of your present corporation or any successor corporation or firm.

Date

Signature of Client
(If More Than One, All Principals to the Account Must Sign)

x _____

x _____

x _____

x _____

b. Confirmation of Trading Authority

I have carefully examined the provisions of the above "trading authorization" by which I have given trading authority or control to _____ and understand fully the obligations which I have assumed by executing that document.

I understand that your corporation is no way responsible for any loss to me occasioned by the actions of the individual or organization named above and that your corporation does not, by implication or otherwise, endorse the operating methods of such individual organization. I further understand that the Chicago Board of Trade or Chicago Mercantile Exchange has no jurisdiction over a non-member who is not employed by one of its members and that if I give to such individual or organization authority to exercise any of my rights over my account I do so at my own risk.

In addition, I am aware that if my agent is not my spouse, parent, child or grandparent the regulations of the Chicago Board of Trade require the maintenance of a minimum net equity on Chicago Board of Trade commodities of not less than $5,000.

Date

Signature
(If More Than One, All Principals to the Account Must Sign)

x _____

x _____

x _____

x _____

Exhibit 10–3
Client Information Sheet
Individual or Sole Proprietorship

Check one   Account No. _____

☐ Individual Account

☐ Sole Proprietorship Account
                                        ☐ Miss
Please print or type   ☐ Mrs.
                                        ☐ Dr.
Name of Individual   ☐ Mr. _____

If Sole Proprietor Account, Name under which conducted _____

Customer Account Title _____

Mailing Address (for all statements and notices) If floor trader, indicate exchange floor		Home Address (if different)	
Street or P.O. Box			
City			
State	Zip	Home Telephone	
Age _____ Date of Birth _____		Place of Birth _____	
Social Security No. _____		Federal ID No. (if applicable) _____	

Employer's Name, Address and Telephone			
Name		Position	
Street		Title	
		Direct work phone	
City	State	Zip	
Phone			

Bank References			
	Officer		Officer
Street		Street	
City	State	Zip	City	State	Zip

1. Have you ever had a commodity account before? (If YES, please identify firm, branch and account number)   YES ☐   NO ☐

2. Do you have pending litigation, disputed accounts, or other unresolved matters with commodity or security brokers at this time? (If YES, please briefly describe)   YES ☐   NO ☐

3. Will this account be traded on your behalf by someone else? (If YES, please complete and attach Power of Attorney form)   YES ☐   NO ☐

4. Are funds in this account to be used for the benefit of another? (If YES, give name and address of such person(s) or entity)   YES ☐   NO ☐

5. Does this account and/or person(s) control or have financial interest in the trading of any other account(s) with this firm? (If YES, give name and number of other account(s))   YES ☐   NO ☐

Exhibit 10–3, *Concluded*
Client Information Sheet
Individual or Sole Proprietorship

6. Does any other person(s) and/or account(s):
   A. Control the trading of this account?   YES ☐   NO ☐

   B. Have any financial interest in this account?   YES ☐   NO ☐

   C. Guarantee this account? (If YES, give name(s) of person(s) and designate account(s))   YES ☐   NO ☐

   _____

   _____

   _____

7. Have you ever been subject to federal or state bankruptcy proceedings, receivership or similar proceedings (voluntarily or involuntarily)?   YES ☐   NO ☐

   (If YES, describe briefly.) _____

   _____

The following financial statement is made as of _____
                                               Date

Assets		Liabilities and Net Worth	
Cash, Deposits	_____	Accounts, Notes, Loans Payable	_____
Other Liquid Assets	_____	Taxes Payable	_____
Securities	_____	Mortgages Payable on Real Estate	_____
Residence (Mkt. Value)	_____	Exchange Membership Loans	_____
Other Real Estate	_____	Other Liabilities	_____
Exchange Memberships	_____	Total Liabilities	_____
Other Assets	_____		
		Net Worth	_____
Total Assets	_____	Total Liabilities and Net Worth	_____

Are any of the above assets pledged? Yes ☐ No ☐ if YES, list: _____

Contingent Liabilities _____
(i.e. personal guarantees, etc.)

Approximate Gross   Average Annual
Annual Income _____   Gross Income
                           last 3 years _____

Client Signature _____ Date _____

Exhibit 10–3A
Client Agreement for Individual or Sole Proprietorship

In consideration of the acceptance by CSA, Inc. ("Broker") of one or more accounts of the undersigned client and its agreement to act as broker for the undersigned in the purchase and sale of commodities futures contracts, the undersigned agrees as follows:

1. Client authorizes Broker to purchase and sell commodities futures contracts for Client's account in accordance with the oral or written instructions of Client or Client's designated trading advisor. All orders from Client to buy or sell commodities futures contracts must be complete and contain the following information:

   (a) Client's identity and account number;
   (b) Commodity;
   (c) Quantity;
   (d) Price, if applicable;
   (e) Contract delivery month;
   (f) Any unique aspects of order.

2. Client shall deposit with Broker sufficient funds to meet the applicable initial and maintenance margin requirements. Client shall, without notice or demand, maintain adequate margins at all times so as to continuously meet the margin requirements established by Broker. Broker may establish margin requirements in its sole and absolute discretion and said requirements may exceed the margin requirements set by any commodity exchange or other regulatory authority. Client agrees, when requested by Broker, to immediately wire transfer funds to adequately maintain margins and to furnish Broker with the names of bank officers for immediate confirmation of such transfers. Failure to demand wire transfer of funds or the acceptance of funds by mail shall not constitute a waiver of the right of Broker to demand wire transfer of funds at any time.

3. If at any time Client account does not contain the amount of margin required, Broker may, in its sole and absolute discretion, without notice or demand to Client, close out Client's open positions in whole or in part or take any other action it deems necessary to satisfy such margin requirements. Failure of Broker to act in such circumstances shall not constitute a waiver of its rights to do so at any time thereafter, nor shall Broker be subject to any liability to Client for its failure to so act.

4. Broker is financially liable to the exchange clearing houses of which it is a member and to the clearing members through which it clears transactions on exchanges of which it is not a clearing member, for maintenance margins and deficit balances occuring in Client's account making Broker, in effect, the guarantor of the financial responsibility of Client. Client agrees to indemnify and hold Broker harmless against and from any and all losses, costs and damages (including costs and attorneys' fees incurred in collecting such deficit) sustained by Broker resulting, directly or indirectly, from any action or omission by Client with respect to the account(s), including, but not limited to, any deficit balances which may occur in Client's account.

5. Client agrees to pay, to Broker, commission charges in effect from time to time, and any other costs to Broker occasioned by carrying the account of Client. Client agrees to pay the amount of any deficit balance that may result from transactions executed by Broker for Client's account and to pay the interest and service charges on any deficit balances at the rates customarily charged by Broker, together with any expenses incurred by Broker, including court costs and attorneys' fees incurred in collecting any such deficit. All such payments shall be made within twenty-four (24) hours following Client's receipt of Broker's request for payment (except as modified with respect to wire and telephonic requests for margin funds as herein set forth).

6. All monies, securities, negotiable instruments, open positions in futures contracts and commodities, or other property now or at any future time held in Client's account or which may be in Broker's possession for any purpose, including safekeeping, shall be subject to a general lien and security interest for the discharge of all obligations of Client to Broker, irrespective of whether or not Broker has made advances in connection with such securities, futures contracts, commodities or other property, and irrespective of the number of accounts Client may have with Broker. Broker may, at any time, in its sole and absolute discretion, liquidate any of the above-mentioned items in order to satisfy any margin or account deficiencies of Client and may transfer said property or assets to the general ledger account of Broker, all without liability on the part of Broker to Client or any third party.

7. If, at any time, Client shall be unable to deliver to Broker any security, commodity or other property previously sold by Broker on Client's behalf, Client authorizes Broker, in Broker's sole discretion, to borrow or buy and deliver the same, and Client shall immediately pay and indemnify Broker for any costs, loss and damage (including consequential costs, losses and damages) which Broker may sustain in making such delivery together with any premiums which Broker may be required to pay and for any costs, loss, and damage (including consequential costs, losses, and damages) which Broker may sustain from its inability to borrow or buy any such security, commodity or other property. In the event Broker takes delivery of any security or commodity for Client's account, Client agrees to indemnify and hold Broker harmless from and against any loss it may suffer resulting, directly or indirectly, from a decline in value of said security or commodity.

8. Client acknowledges that (a) any market recommendations or information communicated to Client by Broker do not constitute an offer to sell or the solicitation of an offer to buy any commodity futures contract; (b) such recommendations and information, although based upon information obtained from sources believed by Broker to be reliable, may be incomplete and unverified; and (c) Broker makes no representation, warranty or guarantee as to, and shall not be responsible for the accuracy or completeness of, any information or trading recommendation furnished to Client. Client understands that Broker, its affiliates or representatives, may have a position in and may intend to buy or sell commodities, or commodity future contracts which are the subject of market recommendations furnished to Client, and that the market position of Broker or any such affiliate or representative may or may not be consistent with the recommendations furnished to Client by Broker.

9. All transactions under this Agreement shall be subject to the applicable constitution, rules, regulations, customs, usages, rulings and interpretations of the exchanges or markets on which such transactions are executed by Broker for Client's account and, where applicable, to the provisions of the Commodity Exchange Act, as amended, and the rules and regulations promulgated thereunder and to any other applicable governmental statutes, rules and regulations.

10. All orders placed by Client or Client's designated trading advisor may be executed on any exchange or other place where such business is transacted and, unless otherwise specified, Broker is authorized to execute such orders upon any exchange or other place which may be deemed by Broker, in its sole discretion, to be most desirable.

11. In the event of (a) Client's death or legal incapacity; (b) the filing of a petition in bankruptcy by or against Client; (c) the institution of any similar state, federal or other insolvency proceeding by or against Client; (d) the appointment of a receiver for the Client or of any assets of Client; (e) an attachment is levied against Client's account (or any of them); (f) a notice of levy with respect to Client's account (or any of them) is served on Broker by any competent taxing authority; (g) Client fails to meet any margin calls, or (h) Broker deems itself for any reason insecure, ther, Broker is hereby authorized, in its sole discretion, to sell any or all of the commodity futures contracts, commodities or other property of Client which may be in Broker's possession, or which Broker may be carrying for Client, or to buy in any commodity futures contracts, commodities or other property of which the account or accounts of Client

Exhibit 10–3A, *Concluded*
Client Agreement for Individual or Sole Proprietorship

may be short, or cancel any outstanding orders in order to close out the account or accounts of Client in whole or in part in order to close out any commitment made on behalf of Client, all without any liability on the part of Broker to Client or any third party. Such sale, purchase or cancellation may be made according to Broker's judgment and may be made at its discretion, on the exchange or other market where such business is usually transacted, without notice to Client or the legal representative of Client, and without prior tender, demand or call of any kind upon Client or the legal representative of Client, and Broker may purchase the whole or any part thereof free from any right of redemption, and Client shall remain liable for any deficiency, it being understood that a prior tender, demand or call of any kind from Broker, or prior notice from Broker, of time and place of such sale or purchase shall not be considered a waiver of Broker's right to sell or buy any commodity futures contracts, commodities or other property held by Broker or owned by Client, at any time as hereinbefore provided or to be deemed to require any such tender, demand, call or notice on any subsequent transaction.

12. All communications, reports, statements, monies, securities, negotiable instruments, and other property shall be mailed or otherwise transmitted to Client at Client's account mailing address as shown on the Client Information Sheet or to such other address as Client may have theretofore designated in writing, and all communications so sent, whether by mail, telegraph, messenger or otherwise, shall be deemed received by Client personally at the time so sent whether actually received or not.

13. Broker shall not be responsible for any loss or damage caused, directly or indirectly, by any events, actions or omissions beyond the control of Broker, including, without limitation, loss or damage resulting, directly or indirectly, from any delays or inaccuracies in the transmission of orders or other information due to a breakdown in or failure of any transmission or communication facilities.

14. Reports of executions and all statements of account rendered by Broker from time to time to Client shall be conclusively deemed correct and final, unless Client gives written notice to the contrary, within two (2) days in the case of reports of executions, and within ten (10) days in the case of statements of account. Margin calls shall be conclusively deemed correct and final if not objected to immediately by telephone or wire.

15. If any part, term or provision of this Agreement is held by any body of competent jurisdiction to be illegal or in conflict with the law of any state or any other law, the validity of the remaining portions or provisions shall not be affected, and the rights and obligations of the parties shall be construed and enforced as if this Agreement did not contain the particular part, term or provision held to be invalid.

16. This Agreement, including all authorizations, shall inure to the benefit of Broker, its successors and assigns and shall be binding upon Client and Client's personal representatives, executors, trustees, administrators, successors and assigns.

17. This Agreement may be prospectively altered, modified or amended by Broker from time to time by written notice to Client. No other modification, amendment or addition to this Agreement shall be effective unless reduced to writing and signed by both Client and Broker. This instrument embodies the entire Agreement of the parties, superseding any and all prior agreements and there are no other terms, conditions or obligations other than those contained herein.

18. Client represents, warrants and agrees that; (a) Client is under no legal disability and no one except Client will have an interest in Client's account with Broker; (b) all of the information contained in the Client Information Sheet is true, complete and correct as of the date hereof and that the undersigned will promptly notify the Broker of any changes therein; (c) the account carried on the books of Broker is organized as a sole proprietorship of which Client is the sole proprietor (if applicable). The Client agrees to indemnify and hold CSA, Inc., its successors and assigns, harmless against and from any and all loss, damage or liability incurred because any of the above representations or warranties shall, at any time, not be true and correct or the covenants herein contained shall not have been fully performed by the Client.

19. Client authorizes Broker to contact such banks, financial institutions and credit agencies as Broker shall deem appropriate from time to time to verify the information regarding Client which may be provided by Client from time to time.

20. Client, in order to induce Broker to accept this Client Agreement, and for other good and valuable consideration, the receipt and sufficiency of which is hereby acknowledged, hereby consents to the jurisdiction of any local, state or federal court located within the State of Illinois in connection with all suits, actions or other legal proceedings commenced by or for the benefit of Broker arising directly, indirectly or otherwise in connection with, out of, related to or from Client's account, transactions contemplated by this Client Agreement or breach thereof, Client hereby waiving any and all objections Client may, at any time, have as to the propriety of the Court in which any such suits, actions or proceedings may be commenced, as aforesaid.

21. Any controversy between Broker and Client shall be settled by arbitration at Chicago, Illinois in accordance with the rules then and there obtaining of either the American Arbitration Association, or the Board of Arbitration of any organized market or Board of Trade, or exchange of which Broker is a member and upon which the transaction was executed, as Client may elect. If Client does not elect by registered mail addressed to Broker at its main office within five (5) days after receipt of notification asking for election, Client authorizes Broker to make such election in behalf of Client. Any award given before and by the arbitrators shall be final, and a judgment upon the award rendered may be entered in any court, state or federal, having jurisdiction.

Client Signature _____ Date _____

OFFICE USE ONLY

Approved by:

Officer _____

Officer _____

Dated: _____

Exhibit 10–3B
Risk Disclosure Statement for Individual or Sole Proprietorship

This statement is furnished to you because rule 1.55 of the Commodity Futures Trading Commission requires it.

The risk of loss in trading commodity futures contracts can be substantial. You should therefore carefully consider whether such trading is suitable for you in light of your financial condition. In considering whether to trade, you should be aware of the following:

(1) You may sustain a total loss of the initial margin funds and any additional funds that you deposit with your broker to establish or maintain a position in the commodity futures market. If the market moves against your position, you may be called upon by your broker to deposit a substantial amount of additional margin funds, on short notice, in order to maintain your position. If you do not provide the required funds within the prescribed time, your position may be liquidated at a loss, and you will be liable for any resulting deficit in your account.

(2) Under certain market conditions, you may find it difficult or impossible to liquidate a position. This can occur, for example, when the market makes a "limit move."

(3) Placing contingent orders, such as "stop-loss" or "stop-limit" order, will not necessarily limit your losses to the intended amounts, since market conditions may make it impossible to execute such orders.

(4) A "spread" position may not be less risky than a simple "long" or "short" position.

(5) The high degree of leverage that is often obtainable in futures trading because of the small margin requirements can work against you as well as for you. The use of leverage can lead to large losses as well as gains.

This brief statement cannot, of course, disclose all the risks and other significant aspects of the commodity markets. You should therefore carefully study futures trading before you trade.

The undersigned acknowledges that he has received and understands the foregoing Risk Disclosure Statement prior to opening a commodities account with CSA, Inc.

Date   Signature of Client

_____   x _____

Witness

x _____

Exhibit 10–3C
Authorization to Transfer Funds for Individual or Sole Proprietorship

Until further notice in writing you are authorized, at any time and from time to time, without prior notice to the undersigned, to transfer from my Regulated Commodity Account to any other account held by you for me, such excess funds, equities, securities, and/or other property as in your judgment may be required for margin, to avoid the calling of margin on open trades in Unregulated Commodities or Securities, or to reduce any debit balance or to reduce and/or satisfy any deficits in such other security and/or commodity accounts. By "Regulated Commodity" is meant any commodity covered by the Commodity Exchange Act at the time of such transaction.

You agree, however, that within a reasonable time after making such transfer you will confirm the same in writing to the undersigned.

Date   Signature of Client

_____   _____

Exhibit 10–4
Client Information Sheet
Partnership or Joint Account

Check one

☐ General Partnership Account   Account No. _____
☐ Limited Partnership Account
☐ Joint Account (with right of survivorship)

Please print or type*

──────────────── PARTNERSHIP ACCOUNT ────────────────

Name(s) of General Partner(s) _____ (1)
_____ (2)
_____ (3)
_____ (4)
Partnership Account Title _____
Managing General Partner Name and Address _____
(Account Mailing Address) _____

Partnership Information
Partnership Address _____
_____ Zip _____
Partnership Phone _____
Partnership Federal ID Number _____
Type of Business _____
Bank Reference _____ Officer _____
Address _____
_____ Zip _____

──────────────── JOINT ACCOUNT ────────────────

Name(s) of Individual(s) _____ (1)
_____ (2)
_____ (3)
Joint Account Title _____
Account Mailing Address _____
_____

Individual Information   Individual (1)
Occupation _____   Home Address _____
Employer's Name and Address _____   _____
_____   _____ Zip _____
_____ Zip _____   Home Phone _____
Employer's Telephone _____   Age _____ Date of Birth _____
Direct Work Phone _____   Place of Birth _____
Bank Reference _____ Officer _____   Social Security Number _____
Address _____   Federal ID No. (If applicable) _____
_____ Zip _____
*If the space provided for any answer is insufficient, attach additional sheet(s), initialed by Clients.
                                                 Individual (2)
Occupation _____   Home Address _____
Employer's Name and Address _____   _____
_____   _____ Zip _____
_____ Zip _____   Home Phone _____
Employer's Telephone _____   Age _____ Date of Birth _____
Direct Work Phone _____   Place of Birth _____
Bank Reference _____ Officer _____   Social Security Number _____
Address _____   Federal ID No. (If applicable) _____
_____ Zip _____

Exhibit 10–4, *Concluded*
Client Information Sheet
Partnership or Joint Account

Individual (3)

Occupation _____   Home Address _____
Employer's Name and Address _____
_____   _____ Zip _____
_____ Zip _____   Home Phone _____
Employer's Telephone _____   Age _____ Date of Birth _____
Direct Work Phone _____   Place of Birth _____
Bank Reference _____ Officer _____   Social Security Number _____
Address _____   Federal ID No. (If applicable) _____
_____ Zip _____

──────────────── **GENERAL INFORMATION** (All Accounts)* ────────────────

The following financial statement is made as of _____

ASSETS		LIABILITIES AND NET WORTH	
	date		
Cash, Deposits	_____	Accounts, Loans, Notes Payable	_____
Other Liquid Assets	_____	Taxes Payable	_____
Securities	_____	Mortgages Payable on Real Estate	_____
Real Estate (Market Value)	_____	Exchange Membership Loans Outstanding	_____
Exchange Memberships	_____	Other Liabilities	_____
Other Assets	_____	Total Liabilities	_____
		Net Worth	_____
Total Assets	_____	Total Liabilities and Net Worth	_____

Contingent Liabilities _____
(i.e. personal guarantees, etc.)

Are any of the above assets pledged? YES ☐   NO ☐   If YES, list _____
Approximate Gross Annual Income _____   Average Annual Gross Income Over Last 3 years _____

Have any of you ever been subject to federal or state bankruptcy proceedings, receivership or similar proceedings   YES ☐   NO ☐
(voluntarily or involuntarily)?

(If YES, describe briefly) _____

1. Have any of you ever had a commodity account before? (IF YES, please give name and identify firm, branch and account   YES ☐   NO ☐
number)
_____
_____

2. Do any of you have pending litigation, disputed accounts, or other unresolved matters between commodity or security   YES ☐   NO ☐
brokers at this time? (If YES, please briefly describe)
_____
_____

3. Will this account be traded on behalf of this entity by someone else? (If YES, please complete and attach Power of   YES ☐   NO ☐
Attorney form)

4. Are funds in this account to be used for the benefit of another? (If YES, give name and address of such person(s) or   YES ☐   NO ☐
entity)
_____
_____

5. Does this account and/or person(s) control or have financial interest in the trading of any other account(s) with this firm?   YES ☐   NO ☐
If YES, give name and number of other account(s)
_____
_____

6. Do(es) any other person(s) and/or account(s):
  A. Control the trading of this account?   YES ☐   NO ☐
  B. Have any financial interest in this account?   YES ☐   NO ☐
  C. Guarantee this account? If YES, give name(s) of person(s) and designate account(s)   YES ☐   NO ☐
_____

Client Signature (All parties listed must sign)   Date

Exhibit 10–4A
Client Agreement for Partnership or Joint Account

In consideration of the acceptance by CSA, Inc. ("Broker") of one or more accounts of the undersigned ("Client") and its agreement to act as broker for the undersigned in the purchase and sale of commodities futures contracts, the undersigned agrees as follows.

1. Client authorizes Broker to purchase and sell commodities futures contracts for Client's account in accordance with the oral or written instructions of Client or Client's designated trading advisor. All orders from Client to buy or sell commodities futures contracts must be complete and contain the following information: (a) Client's identity and account number; (b) Commodity; (c) Quantity; (d) Price, if applicable; (e) Contract delivery month; (f) Any unique aspects of order.

2. Client shall deposit with Broker sufficient funds to meet the applicable initial and maintenance margin requirements. Client shall, without notice or demand, maintain adequate margins at all times so as to continuously meet the margin requirements established by Broker. Broker may establish margin requirements in its sole and absolute discretion and said requirements may exceed the margin requirements set by any commodity exchange or other regulatory authority. Client agrees, when requested by Broker, to immediately wire transfer funds to adequately maintain margins and to furnish Broker with the names of bank officers for immediate confirmation of such transfers. Failure to demand wire transfer of funds or the acceptance of funds by mail shall not constitute a waiver of the right of Broker to demand wire transfer of funds at any time.

3. If at any time Client's account does not contain the amount of margin required, Broker may, in its sole and absolute discretion, without notice or demand to Client, close out Client's open positions in whole or in part or take any other action it deems necessary to satisfy such margin requirements. Failure of Broker to act in such circumstances shall not constitute a waiver of its rights to do so at any time thereafter, nor shall Broker be subject to any liability to Client for its failure to so act.

4. Broker is financially liable to the exchange clearing houses of which it is a member and to the clearing members through which it clears transactions on exchanges of which it is not a clearing member for maintenance margins and deficit balances occurring in Client's account making Broker, in effect, the guarantor of the financial responsibility of Client. Client agrees to indemnify and hold Broker harmless against and from any and all losses, costs and damages (including costs and attorneys' fees incurred in collecting such deficit) sustained by Broker resulting, directly or indirectly, from any action or omission by Client with respect to the account(s), including, but not limited to, any deficit balances which may occur in Client's account.

5. Client agrees to pay, to Broker, commission charges in effect from time to time, and any other costs occasioned by carrying the account of Client. Client agrees to pay the amount of any deficit balance that may result from transactions executed by Broker for Client's account and to pay the interest and service charges on any deficit balances at the rates customarily charged by Broker, together with any expenses incurred by Broker, including court costs and attorneys' fees incurred in collecting any such deficit. All such payments shall be made within twenty-four (24) hours following Client's receipt of Broker's request for payment (except as modified with respect to wire and telephonic requests for margin funds as herein set forth).

6. All monies, securities, negotiable instruments, open positions in futures contracts and commodities, or other property now or at any future time held in Client's account or which may be in Broker's possession for any purpose, including safekeeping, shall be subject to a general lien and security interest for the discharge of all obligations of Client to Broker, irrespective of whether or not Broker has made advances in connection with such securities, futures contracts, commodities or other property, and irrespective of the number of accounts Client may have with Broker. Broker may, at any time, in its sole and absolute discretion, liquidate any of the above-mentioned items in order to satisfy any margin or account deficiencies of Client and may transfer said property or assets to the general ledger account of Broker, all without liability on the part of Broker to Client or any third party.

7. If, at any time, Client shall be unable to deliver to Broker any security, commodity or other property previously sold by Broker on Client's behalf, Client authorizes Broker, in Broker's sole discretion, to borrow or buy and deliver the same, and Client shall immediately pay and indemnify Broker for any costs, loss and damage (including consequential costs, losses and damages) which Broker may sustain in making such delivery together with any premiums which Broker may be required to pay and for any costs, loss, and damage (including consequential costs, losses, and damages) which Broker may sustain from its inability to borrow or buy any such security, commodity or other property. In the event Broker takes delivery of any security or commodity for Client's account, Client agrees to indemnify and hold Broker harmless against and from any loss it may suffer resulting, directly or indirectly, from a decline in value of said security or commodity.

8. Client acknowledges that (a) any market recommendations or information communicated to Client by Broker do not constitute an offer to sell or the solicitation of an offer to buy any commodity futures contract; (b) such recommendations and information, although based upon information obtained from sources believed by Broker to be reliable, may be incomplete and unverified; and (c) Broker makes no representation, warranty or guarantee as to, and shall not be responsible for the accuracy or completeness of, any information or trading recommendation furnished to Client. Client understands that Broker, its affiliates or representatives, may have a position in and may intend to buy or sell commodities or commodity future contracts which are the subject of market recommendations furnished to Client, and that the market position of Broker or any such affiliate or representative may or may not be consistent with the recommendations furnished to Client by Broker.

9. All transactions under this agreement shall be subject to the applicable constitution, rules, regulations, customs, usages, rulings and interpretations of the exchanges or markets on which such transactions are executed by Broker for Client's account and, where applicable, to the provisions of the Commodity Exchange Act, as amended, and the rules and regulations promulgated thereunder and to any other applicable governmental statutes, rules and regulations.

10. All orders placed by Client or Client's designated trading advisor may be executed on any exchange or other place where such business is transacted and, unless otherwise specified, Broker is authorized to execute such orders upon any exchange or other place which may be deemed by Broker, in its sole discretion, to be most desirable.

11. In the event of (a) where client is a general or limited partnership, the partnership is to be dissolved or in the case of a Joint Account, the death of the last survivor thereof; (b) the filing of a petition in bankruptcy by or against Client; (c) the institution of any similar state, federal or other insolvency proceedings by or against Client; (d) the appointment of a receiver for Client or any of the assets of Client; (e) an attachment is levied against Client's account (or any of them); (f) a notice of levy with respect to Client's account (or any of them) is served on Broker by any competent taxing authority; (g) Client fails to meet any margin calls; (h) Broker deems itself for any reason insecure, then Broker is hereby authorized, in its sole discretion, to sell any or all of the commodity futures contracts, commodities or other property of Client which may be in Broker's possession, or which Broker may be carrying for Client, or to buy in any commodity futures contracts, commodities or other property of which the account or accounts of Client may be short, or cancel any outstanding orders in order to close out the account or accounts of Client in whole or in part in order to close out any commitment made on behalf of Client, all without any liability on the part of Broker to Client or any third party. Such sale, purchase or cancellation may be made according to Broker's judgment and may be made at its discretion, on the exchange or other market where such business is usually transacted, without notice to Client or the legal representative of Client, and without prior tender, demand or call of any kind upon Client or the legal representative of Client, and Broker may purchase the whole or any part thereof free from any right of redemption, and Client shall remain liable for any deficiency, it being understood that a prior tender, demand or call of any kind from Broker, or prior notice from Broker, of the time and place of such sale or purchase shall not be considered a waiver of Broker's right to sell or buy any commodity futures contracts, commodities or other property held by Broker or owned by Client, at any time as hereinbefore provided or to be deemed to require any such tender, demand, call or notice on any subsequent transaction.

12. All communications, reports, statements, monies, securities, negotiable instruments, and other property shall be mailed or otherwise transmitted to Client at Client's account mailing address as shown on the Client Information Sheet or to such other address as Client may have theretofore designated in writing, and all communications so sent, whether by mail, telegraph, messenger or otherwise, shall be deemed received by Client personally at the time so sent whether actually received or not.

13. Broker shall not be responsible for any loss or damage caused, directly or indirectly, by any events, actions or omissions beyond the control of Broker, including, without limitation, loss or damage resulting, directly or indirectly, from any delays or inaccuracies in the transmission of orders or other information due to a breakdown in or failure of any transmission or communication facilities.

14. Reports of executions and all statements of account rendered by Broker from time to time to Client shall be deemed conclusively correct and final, unless Client gives written notice to the contrary, within two (2) days in the case of reports of executions, and within ten (10) days in the case of statements of account. Margin calls shall be deemed conclusively correct and final if not objected to immediately by telephone or wire.

15. If any part, term or provision of this Agreement is held by any body of competent jurisdiction to be illegal or in conflict with the law of any state or any other law, the validity of the remaining portions or provisions shall not be affected, and the rights and obligations of the parties shall be construed and enforced as if this Agreement did not contain the particular part, term or provision held to be invalid.

16. This Agreement, including all authorizations, shall inure to the benefit of Broker, its successors and assigns and shall be binding upon Client and Client's legal representatives, executors, trustees, administrators, successors and assigns.

17. This Agreement may be prospectively altered, modified or amended by Broker from time to time by written notice to Client. No other modification, amendment or addition to this Agreement shall be effective unless reduced to writing and signed by both Client and Broker. This instrument embodies the entire Agreement of the parties, superseding any and all prior agreements and there are no other terms, conditions or obligations other than those contained herein.

Exhibit 10–4A, *Concluded*
Client Agreement for Partnership or Joint Account

18. In case of a General or Limited Partnership Account, the undersigned hereby represent that they are all of the general partners in a general partnership or limited partnership, as the case may be, as identified on the Client Information Sheet, and in consideration of Broker opening a commodities account for and in the name of the Partnership, the undersigned hereby jointly and severally agree and consent to the terms of the Client Agreement and represent, warrant and agree that:

    (a) All of the information contained in the Client Information Sheet is true, complete and correct as of the date hereof and that the undersigned will promptly notify Broker of any changes therein;

    (b) The partnership is a duly organized, validly existing partnership under the laws of the state(s) in which it was formed and in which it does business;

    (c) The person identified on the Client Information Sheet as the Managing Partner is a general partner in the Partnership, having a significant interest therein, and is authorized, for the Partnership's account and at its risk, to buy, sell and trade in commodities and commodity futures contracts of every kind whatsoever, or to designate a trading advisor and to borrow money for such purposes in said account in accordance with the terms and conditions of this Client Agreement and related documents. Broker may conclusively assume that all actions taken, and instructions given, by the said Managing Partner have been properly taken or given pursuant to authority vested in said Managing Partner by all of the partners in the Partnership. Broker is authorized to follow the instructions of the said Managing Partner in every respect concerning said account, and to make payment of monies as he may order and direct and to send to him all reports, confirmations, statements and notices relating to the account; provided, however, that no payments shall be made by Broker except in the name of the Partnership. The said Managing Partner is authorized to execute and deliver on behalf of the Partnership and its members any agreements Broker may require, and to act for the Partnership and its members in every respect concerning said account and to do all other things necessary or incidental to the conduct of said account, including the designation of any attorney or attorneys-in-fact, all as fully and completely as if he alone were interested in said account. If new partners are admitted to the Partnership, the undersigned will cause such new members to adopt and be bound by this Client Agreement and related documents; and

    (d) The Articles of Partnership or Limited Partnership, as the case may be, are in writing and provide that the Partnership will not terminate upon the death or incapacity of any one of the partners.

18a. In the case of a Joint Account, Client jointly and severally represents, warrants and agrees that:

    (a) All of the information contained in the Client Information Sheet is true, complete and correct as of the date hereof and that the undersigned will promptly notify Broker of any changes therein;

    (b) None of the undersigned are under any legal disability and no one other than those indicated on the Client Information Sheet has any interest in this Joint Account;

    (c) Any one of the undersigned shall have full authority (i) to give any instructions with respect to the account(s), including but not limited to instructions with respect to buying or selling or withdrawals of excess funds; (ii) to receive any demands, notices, confirmations, reports, statements and other communications of any kind; (iii) generally to deal with Broker in connection herewith as fully and completely as if the other joint tenant or tenants had no interest herein; and

    (d) Broker shall be under no duty or obligation to enquire into the purpose or propriety of any instruction given and shall be under no obligation to see the application of any funds delivered by Client in respect of the account(s).

19. The Client agrees to indemnify and hold CSA, Inc. its successors and assigns, harmless against and from any and all loss, damage or liability incurred because any of the above representations or warranties shall, at any time, not be true and correct or the covenants herein contained shall not have been fully performed by the client.

20. Client shall promptly notify Broker, in writing, of the death or retirement of any of the General Partners or any material change in the appropriate partnership agreement, in the case of a general or Limited Partnership Account, or the death of any of the signatories to a Joint Account, as the case may be.

21. For purposes of this Agreement and notwithstanding any expression or inference herein to the contrary, as used herein, the term "Client" shall include each and every signatory hereto (other than Broker), the parties intending hereby to create joint and several liability on the part of said signatories for the full performance and fulfillment of all of the duties, obligations, covenants, representations and warranties of Customer hereunder and for the breach of any of them.

22. Client authorizes Broker to contact such banks, financial institutions and credit agencies as Broker shall deem appropriate from time to time to verify the information regarding Client which may be provided by Client from time to time.

23. Client, in order to induce Broker to accept this Client Agreement, and for other good and valuable consideration, the receipt and sufficiency of which is hereby acknowledged, hereby consents to the jurisdiction of any local, state or federal court located within the State of Illinois in connection with all suits, actions or other legal proceedings commenced by or for the benefit of Broker arising directly, indirectly or otherwise in connection with, out of, related to or from Client's account, transactions contemplated by this Client Agreement or breach thereof. Client hereby waiving any and all objections Client may, at any time, have as to the propriety of the Court in which any such suits, actions or proceedings may be commenced, as aforesaid.

24. Any controversy between Broker and Client shall be settled by arbitration at Chicago, Illinois in accordance with the rules then and there obtaining of either the American Arbitration Association, or the Board of Arbitration of any organized market or Board of Trade, or exchange of which Broker is a member and upon which the transaction was executed, as Client may elect. If Client does not elect by registered mail addressed to Broker at its main office within five (5) days after receipt of notification asking for election, Client authorizes Broker to make such election in behalf of Client. Any award given before and by the arbitrators shall be final, and a judgment upon the award rendered may be entered in any court, state or federal, having jurisdiction.

Partnership Account
CLIENT (All General Partners Must Sign)

    Joint Account
CLIENT (All persons named in Client Information Sheet Must Sign)

By_____
    A General Partner   Date
    _____ Date

By_____
    A General Partner   Date
    _____ Date

By_____
    A General Partner   Date
    _____ Date

By_____
    A General Partner   Date
    _____ Date

OFFICE USE ONLY

Approved by_____

Officer(s)_____

Officer(s)_____ Date_____

Exhibit 10–4B
Risk Disclosure Statement for Partnership or Joint Account

This statement is furnished to you because rule 1.55 of the Commodity Futures Trading Commission requires it.

The risk of loss in trading commodity futures contracts can be substantial. You should therefore carefully consider whether such trading is suitable for you in light of your financial condition. In considering whether to trade, you should be aware of the following:

(1) You may sustain a total loss of the initial margin funds and any additional funds that you deposit with your broker to establish or maintain a position in the commodity futures market. If the market moves against your position, you may be called upon by your broker to deposit a substantial amount of additional margin funds, on short notice, in order to maintain your position. If you do not provide the required funds within the prescribed time, your position may be liquidated at a loss, and you will be liable for any resulting deficit in your account.

(2) Under certain market conditions, you may find it difficult or impossible to liquidate a position. This can occur, for example, when the market makes a "limit move."

(3) Placing contingent orders, such as "stop-loss" or "stop-limit" order, will not necessarily limit your losses to the intended amounts, since market conditions may make it impossible to execute such orders.

(4) A "spread" position may not be less risky than a simple "long" or "short" position.

(5) The high degree of leverage that is often obtainable in futures trading because of the small margin requirements can work against you as well as for you. The use of leverage can lead to large losses as well as gains.

This brief statement cannot, of course, disclose all the risks and other significant aspects of the commodity markets. You should therefore carefully study futures trading before you trade.

The undersigned acknowledges that he has received and understands the foregoing Risk Disclosure Statement prior to opening a commodities account with CSA, Inc.

Date

Signature of Client

_____   x _____

Witness

x _____

Exhibit 10–4C
Authorization to Transfer Funds for Partnership or Joint Account

Until further notice in writing you are authorized, at any time and from time to time, without prior notice to the undersigned, to transfer from our Regulated Commodity Account to any other account held by you for us, such excess funds, equities, securities, and/or other property as in your judgment may be required for margin, to avoid the calling of margin on open trades in Unregulated Commodities or Securities, or to reduce any debit balance or to reduce and/or satisfy any deficits in such other security and/or commodity accounts. By "Regulated Commodity" is meant any commodity covered by the Commodity Exchange Act at the time of such transaction.

You agree, however, that within a reasonable time after making such transfer you will confirm the same in writing to the undersigned.

Date

Signature of Client
(If More Than One, All Principals to the Account Must Sign)

_____   x _____

x _____

x _____

x _____

Exhibit 10–5
Client Information Sheet
Corporate or Trust

Check one
☐ Corporate Account   Account No. _____
☐ Trust Account

Please print or type*

─────────────────── CORPORATE ACCOUNT ───────────────────
(Complete and attach Corporate Resolutions)

Name of Corporation _____

Corporate Account Title _____

Address of
Principal   _____   State of Incorporation _____
Office
                 _____   Corporate Phone _____

Name of officer, _____   Federal ID Number _____
director or
employee   Bank Reference: _____
authorized to act
with regard to this Phone: _____   Address: _____
Account:
Mailing   Corporate Account: _____   Officer: _____
address
if other than   _____   Trade Reference: _____
principal office
                 _____   Address: _____

                 Attn: _____   Officer: _____

─────────────────── TRUST ACCOUNT ───────────────────

Name of Trust _____   Date _____

Trust Number _____   Date of Trust Creation _____

Federal ID Number _____

Trustee(s)   _____ (1)
              _____ (2)
              _____ (3)

Address of
Trustee(s)   _____ (1)   _____ (2)   _____ (3)
(principal office in
case of corporate   _____   _____   _____
trustee)
              _____   _____   _____

Phone:

Trust Account Title: _____
Trust
Account   _____
Mailing
Address if other _____
than address of
trustee   _____

Phone: _____

*If the space provided for any answer is insufficient, attach additional sheet(s), initialed by Client

Name(s) of Trustee(s), or other person, authorized to act with regard to Trust account

_____

_____

_____

If applicable, specify whether all, one or any specific number of trustees are required to act on behalf of Trust:

_____

Bank Reference _____

Address _____

Officer _____

Exhibit 10–5, *Concluded*
Client Information Sheet
Corporate or Trust

The following financial statement is made as of _____
                                                        date

ASSETS		LIABILITIES AND NET WORTH	
Cash, Deposits	_____	Accounts, Notes, Loans Payable	_____
Other Liquid Assets	_____	Taxes Payable	_____
Securities	_____	Mortgages Payable on Real Estate	_____
Real Estate	_____	Exchange Membership Loans	_____
Exchange Memberships	_____	Other Liabilities	_____
Other Assets	_____	Total Liabilities	_____
		Total Owners Equity	_____
Total Assets	_____	Total Liabilities and Owners Equity	_____
Contingent Liabilities	_____		
(i.e. personal guarantees, etc.)			

Approximate Gross Annual Income _____   Average Annual Gross Income Over Last 3 years _____

If corporation is an FCM, please include 1FR.

1. Has this entity, its officers, directors or any trustee, as the case may be, ever had a commodity account before? (If YES,   YES ☐   NO ☐
please give name and identify firm branch and account number.)

_____

_____

2. Is there any currently pending litigation, disputed accounts, or other unresolved matters between commodity or security   YES ☐   NO ☐
brokers and this entity or any of its officers, directors or trustees, as the case may be? (If YES, please briefly describe)

_____

_____

3. Will this account be traded on behalf of this entity by someone other than an officer, director, employee or trustee? (If   YES ☐   NO ☐
YES, please complete and attach Power of Attorney form)

4. Are funds in this account to be used for the benefit of another (other than the trust beneficiaries in the case of a Trust   YES ☐   NO ☐
Account)? (If YES, give name and address of such person(s) or entity)

_____

_____

5. Does this account and/or person(s) control or have financial interest in the trading of any other account(s) with this firm?   YES ☐   NO ☐
If YES, give name and number of other account(s)

_____

_____

6. Do(es) any other person(s) and/or account(s):
  A. Control the trading of this account?   YES ☐   NO ☐
  B. Have any financial interest in this account?   YES ☐   NO ☐
  C. Guarantee this account?   YES ☐   NO ☐
      If YES, give name(s) of person(s) and designate account(s)

_____

_____

_____

Client signature
(Corporate Account)
Name of Corporation _____

By _____ Date_____

Title _____

Secretary _____ Date_____

(Trust Account)
Name of Trust _____ Number_____

By _____ Date_____
                        Trustee
By _____ Date_____
                        Trustee
By _____ Date_____
                        Trustee

Exhibit 10–5A
Client Agreement for Corporate or Trust Account

In consideration of the acceptance by CSA, Inc ("Broker") of one or more accounts of the undersigned ("Client") and its agreement to act as broker for the undersigned in the purchase and sale of commodities futures contracts, the undersigned agrees as follows

1   Client authorizes Broker to purchase and sell commodities futures contracts for Client's account in accordance with the oral or written instructions of Client or Client's designated trading advisor All orders from Client to buy or sell commodities futures contracts must be complete and contain the following information (a) Client's identity and account number. (b) Commodity (c) Quantity. (d) Price. if applicable. (e) Contract delivery month. (f) Any unique aspects of order

2   Client shall deposit with Broker sufficient funds to meet the applicable initial and maintenance margin requirements. Client shall, without notice or demand, maintain adequate margins at all times so as to continuously meet the margin requirements established by Broker Broker may establish margin requirements in its sole and absolute discretion and said requirements may exceed the margin requirements set by any commodity exchange or other regulatory authority Client agrees when requested by Broker, to immediately wire transfer funds to adequately maintain margins and to furnish Broker with the names of bank officers for immediate confirmation of such transfers Failure to demand wire transfer of funds or the acceptance of funds by mail shall not constitute a waiver of the right of Broker to demand wire transfer of funds at any time

3   If at any time Client's account does not contain the amount of margin required. Broker may, in its sole and absolute discretion, without notice or demand to Client, close out Client's open positions in whole or in part or take any other action it deems necessary to satisfy such margin requirements. Failure of Broker to act in such circumstances shall not constitute a waiver of its rights to do so at any time thereafter, nor shall Broker be subject to any liability to Client for its failure to so act.

4   Broker is financially liable to the exchange clearing houses of which it is a member and to the clearing members through which it clears transactions on exchanges of which it is not a clearing member, for maintenance margins and deficit balances occurring in Client's account making Broker, in effect, the guarantor of the financial responsibility of Client. Client agrees to indemnify and hold Broker harmless against and from any and all losses, costs and damages (including costs and attorneys' fees incurred in collecting such deficit) sustained by Broker resulting, directly or indirectly, from any action or omission by Client with respect to the account(s), including, but not limited to, any deficit balances which may occur in Client's account

5   Client agrees to pay, to Broker, commission charges in effect from time to time, and any other costs occasioned by carrying the account of Client Client agrees to pay the amount of any deficit balance that may result from transactions executed by Broker for Client's account and to pay the interest and service charges on any deficit balances at the rates customarily charged by Broker together with any expenses incurred by Broker, including court costs and attorneys' fees incurred in collecting any such deficit All such payments shall be made within twenty-four (24) hours following Client's receipt of Broker's request for payment (except as modified with respect to wire and telephonic requests for margin funds as herein set forth)

6   All monies, securities, negotiable instruments, open positions in futures contracts and commodities, or other property now or at any future time held in Client's account or which may be in Broker's possession for any purpose, including safekeeping, shall be subject to a general lien and security interest for the discharge of all obligations of Client to Broker irrespective of whether or not Broker has made advances in connection with such securities, futures contracts, commodities or other property, and irrespective of the number of accounts Client may have with Broker. Broker may, at any time, in its sole and absolute discretion, liquidate any of the above-mentioned items in order to satisfy any margin or account deficiencies of Client and may transfer said property or assets to the general ledger account of Broker, all without liability on the part of Broker to Client or any third party

7   If, at any time, Client shall be unable to deliver to Broker any security, commodity or other property previously sold by Broker on Client's behalf, Client authorizes Broker, in Broker's sole discretion, to borrow or buy and deliver the same, and Client shall immediately pay and indemnify Broker for any costs, loss and damage (including consequential costs, losses and damages) which Broker may sustain in making such delivery together with any premiums which Broker may be required to pay and for any costs, loss, and damage (including consequential costs, losses, and damages) which Broker may sustain from its inability to borrow or buy any such security, commodity or other property. In the event Broker takes delivery of any security or commodity for Client's account, Client agrees to indemnify and hold Broker harmless against and from any loss it may suffer resulting, directly or indirectly, from a decline in value of said security or commodity

8   Client acknowledges that (a) any market recommendations or information communicated to Client by Broker do not constitute an offer to sell or the solicitation of an offer to buy any commodity futures contract; (b) such recommendations and information, although based upon information obtained from sources believed by Broker to be reliable, may be incomplete and unverified, and (c) Broker makes no representation, warranty or guarantee as to, and shall not be responsible for the accuracy or completeness of, any information or trading recommendation furnished to Client. Client understands that Broker, its affiliates or representatives, may have a position in and may intend to buy or sell commodities, or commodity future contracts which are the subject of market recommendations furnished to Client, and that the market position of Broker or any such affiliate or representative may or may not be consistent with the recommendations furnished to Client by Broker

9   All transactions under this agreement shall be subject to the applicable constitution, rules, regulations, customs, usages, rulings and interpretations of the exchanges or markets on which such transactions are executed by Broker for Client's account and, where applicable, to the provisions of the Commodity Exchange Act, as amended, and the rules and regulations promulgated thereunder and to any other applicable governmental statutes, rules and regulations

10 All orders placed by Client or Client's designated trading advisor may be executed on any exchange or other place where such business is transacted and, unless otherwise specified. Broker is authorized to execute such orders upon any exchange or other place which may be deemed by Broker, in its sole discretion, to be most desirable.

11 In the event of (a) termination of the trust, or, in the case of a Corporate Account, a transfer of a majority of the shares of capital stock or a decision to dissolve and/or liquidate by the Corporation; (b) the filing of a petition in bankruptcy by or against Client: (c) the institution of any similar state, federal or other insolvency proceedings by or against Client; (d) the appointment of a receiver for Client or any of the assets of Client, (e) an attachment is levied against Client's account (or any of them); (f) a notice of levy with respect to Client's account (or any of them) is served on Broker by any competent taxing authority. (g) Client fails to meet any margin calls, (h) Broker deems itself for any reason insecure, then Broker is hereby authorized, in its sole discretion, to sell any or all of the commodity futures contracts, commodities or other property of Client which may be in Broker's possession, or which Broker may be carrying for Client, or to buy in any commodity futures contracts, commodities or other property of which the account or accounts of Client may be short, or cancel any outstanding orders in order to close out the account or accounts of Client in whole or in part in order to close out any commitment made on behalf of Client, all without any liability on the part of Broker to Client or any third party. Such sale, purchase or cancellation may be made according to Broker's judgment and may be made at its discretion, on the exchange or other market where such business is usually transacted, without notice to Client, and without prior tender, demand or call of any kind upon Client, and Broker may purchase the whole or any part thereof free from any right of redemption, and Client shall remain liable for any deficiency, it being understood that a prior tender, demand or call of any kind from Broker, or prior notice from Broker, of the time and place of such sale or purchase shall not be considered a waiver of Broker's right to sell or buy any commodity futures contracts, commodities or other property held by Broker or owned by Client, at any time as hereinbefore provided or to be deemed to require any such tender, demand, call or notice on any subsequent transaction

12 All communications, reports, statements, monies, securities, negotiable instruments, and other property shall be mailed or otherwise transmitted to Client at Client's account mailing address as shown on the Client Information Sheet or to such other address as Client may have theretofore designated in writing, and all communications so sent, whether by mail, telegraph, messenger or otherwise, shall be deemed received by Client personally at the time so sent whether actually received or not.

13 Broker shall not be responsible for any loss or damage caused, directly or indirectly, by any events, actions or omissions beyond the control of Broker, including, without limitation, loss or damage resulting, directly or indirectly, from any delays or inaccuracies in the transmission of orders or other information due to a breakdown in or failure of any transmission or communication facilities

14 Reports of executions and all statements of account rendered by Broker from time to time to Client shall be deemed conclusively correct and final, unless Client gives written notice to the contrary, within two (2) days in the case of reports of executions, and within ten (10) days in the case of statements of account. Margin calls shall be deemed conclusively correct and final if not objected to immediately by telephone or wire

15 If any part, term or provision of this Agreement is held by any body of competent jurisdiction to be illegal or in conflict with the law of any state or any other law, the validity of the remaining portions or provisions shall not be affected, and the rights and obligations of the parties shall be construed and enforced as if this Agreement did not contain the particular part, term or provision held to be invalid

16 This Agreement, including all authorizations, shall inure to the benefit of Broker, its successors and assigns and shall be binding upon Client and Client's successors and assigns

Exhibit 10–5A, *Concluded*
Client Agreement for Corporate or Trust Account

17. This Agreement may be prospectively altered, modified or amended by Broker from time to time by written notice to Client. No other modification, amendment or addition to this Agreement shall be effective unless reduced to writing and signed by both Client and Broker. This instrument embodies the entire Agreement of the parties, superseding any and all prior agreements and there are no other terms, conditions or obligations other than those contained herein.

18. In case of a Corporate Account, Client represents, warrants and agrees that

    (a) Client is a corporation duly organized and in good standing under the laws of the state of its incorporation and every state in which it does business;

    (b) All of the information contained on the Client Information Sheet is true, correct and complete as of the date hereof and that the undersigned will promptly notify Broker of any changes therein;

    (c) The trading in commodities and commodities future contracts is within the power of Client and such activity will in no manner contravene the provisions of any statutes, rules or regulations, judgments, orders or decrees or agreements to which the Client is bound or subject;

    (d) The actions of the authorized person designated on the Client Information Sheet to act for Client has been authorized by all necessary or appropriate corporate action, such person has full authority to execute this Client Agreement and all related documents on behalf of Client and to act for Client in all matters regarding Client's account(s) and Broker may at all times rely on the fact of such authority without any duty to investigate into either the authenticity or extent thereof; and

    (e) Client will confirm the matters contained in paragraph 18(d) by supplying Broker, within a reasonable time, with an executed copy of resolutions of the Board of Directors of Client in a form prescribed by Broker.

    (f) In the event the foregoing resolutions are rescinded or amended at any time, or any of the representations and warranties set forth above cease to be true and correct at any time, the Client will promptly notify Broker.

18a. In the case of a Trust Account, Client represents, warrants and agrees that

    (a) Client is a duly formed and existing trust under the laws of the state of its formation and the party(ies) designated as trustee(s) thereof on the Client Information Sheet constitute(s) all of (the only) proper trustee(s) thereof;

    (b) All of the information contained in the Client Information Sheet is true, correct and complete as of the date hereof and that the undersigned will promptly notify Broker of any changes therein;

    (c) The trading in commodities and commodities futures contracts is a proper purpose of Client, is within Client's power and such activity will in no manner contravene the provisions of any statutes, rules or regulations, judgments, orders or decrees or agreements to which Client is bound or subject;

    (d) The person(s) designated on the Client Information Sheet as being those required to act in order to constitute the act of Client have been duly authorized to execute this Client Agreement and all related documents on behalf of Client and to act for Client in all matters regarding Client's account(s) and Broker may at all times rely on the fact of such authority without any duty to investigate into either the authenticity or extent thereof; and

    (e) In the event any of the representations and warranties set forth above cease to be true and correct at any time, the Client will promptly notify Broker.

19. The Client agrees to indemnify and hold CSA, Inc. its successors and assigns, harmless against and from any and all loss, damage or liability incurred because any of the above representations or warranties shall, at any time, not be true and correct or the covenants herein contained shall not have been fully performed by the Client.

20. Client shall immediately notify Broker of any transfer of a majority of its capital stock or any intent on the part of Client to dissolve or, in case of a Trust Account, of the imminent termination of the Trust, the death or resignation of any or all of the trustees or any material change in the trust agreement. In the event that any of the trustees of Client (in the case of a trust account) shall be replaced, or the number of trustees increased, Client shall cause each new trustee to become bound to this and all related documents and agreements in their capacity as trustees.

21. Client authorizes Broker to contact such banks, financial institutions and credit agencies as Broker shall deem appropriate from time to time to verify the information regarding Client which may be provided by Client from time to time.

22. Client, in order to induce Broker to accept this Client Agreement, and for other good and valuable consideration, the receipt and sufficiency of which is hereby acknowledged, hereby consents to the jurisdiction of any local, state or federal court located within the State of Illinois in connection with all suits, actions or other legal proceedings commenced by or for the benefit of Broker arising directly, indirectly or otherwise in connection with, out of, related to or from Client's account, transactions contemplated by this Client Agreement or breach thereof. Client hereby waiving any and all objections Client may, at any time, have as to the propriety of the Court in which any such suits, actions or proceedings may be commenced, as aforesaid.

23. Any controversy between Broker and Client shall be settled by arbitration at Chicago, Illinois in accordance with the rules then and there obtaining of either the American Arbitration Association, or the Board of Arbitration of any organized market or Board of Trade, or exchange of which Broker is a member and upon which the transaction was executed, as Client may elect. If Client does not elect by registered mail addressed to Broker at its main office within five (5) days after receipt of notification asking for election, Client authorizes Broker to make such election in behalf of Client. Any award given before and by the arbitrators shall be final, and a judgment upon the award rendered may be entered in any court, state or federal, having jurisdiction.

Trust Account
Client
Name of Trust_____

                                                                 Number

By_____
                         Trustee   Date

By_____
                         Trustee   Date

By_____
                         Trustee   Date

                       Corporate Account
                       Client
                       Name of Corporation_____

                       By_____
                                                                              Date

                       Secretary_____
(Corporate Seal)   Date

OFFICE USE ONLY

Approved by: Officer _____   Officer _____

Date_____

Exhibit 10–5B
Risk Disclosure Statement for Corporate or Trust Account

This statement is furnished to you because rule 1.55 of the Commodity Futures Trading Commission requires it.

The risk of loss in trading commodity futures contracts can be substantial. You should therefore carefully consider whether such trading is suitable for you in light of your financial condition. In considering whether to trade, you should be aware of the following:

(1)   You may sustain a total loss of the initial margin funds and any additional funds that you deposit with your broker to establish or maintain a position in the commodity futures market. If the market moves against your position, you may be called upon by your broker to deposit a substantial amount of additional margin funds, on short notice, in order to maintain your position. If you do not provide the required funds within the prescribed time, your position may be liquidated at a loss, and you will be liable for any resulting deficit in your account.

(2)   Under certain market conditions, you may find it difficult or impossible to liquidate a position. This can occur, for example, when the market makes a "limit move."

(3)   Placing contingent orders, such as "stop-loss" or "stop-limit" order, will not necessarily limit your losses to the intended amounts, since market conditions may make it impossible to execute such orders.

(4)   A "spread" position may not be less risky than a simple "long" or "short" position.

(5)   The high degree of leverage that is often obtainable in futures trading because of the small margin requirements can work against you as well as for you. The use of leverage can lead to large losses as well as gains.

This brief statement cannot, of course, disclose all the risks and other significant aspects of the commodity markets. You should therefore carefully study futures trading before you trade.

The undersigned acknowledges that he has received and understands the foregoing Risk Disclosure Statement prior to opening a commodities account with CSA, Inc.

Date

_____

Witness

x _____

Signature of Client

Name of Client _____

By _____

By _____

By _____

Exhibit 10–5C
Authorization to Transfer Funds for Corporate or Trust Account

Until further notice in writing you are authorized, at any time and from time to time, without prior notice to the undersigned, to transfer from its Regulated Commodity Account to any other account held by you for it, such excess funds, equities, securities, and/or other property as in your judgment may be required for margin, to avoid the calling of margin on open trades in Unregulated Commodities or Securities, or to reduce any debit balance or to reduce and/or satisfy any deficits in such other security and/or commodity accounts. By "Regulated Commodity" is meant any commodity covered by the Commodity Exchange Act at the time of such transaction.

You agree, however, that within a reasonable time after making such transfer you will confirm the same in writing to the undersigned.

Date

Signature of Client

x _____

x _____

x _____

x _____

Exhibit 10–5D
Certificate of Corporate Resolutions for Corporate or Trust Account

I, _____, do hereby certify that I am the duly elected

and acting Secretary of _____ (The "Corporation"), a corporation

validly existing under the laws of the State of _____, and I do further
certify that the following resolutions were duly adopted by the Board of Directors of the Corporation in accordance with applicable

statutes and the Corporation's Charter and By-laws on the _____ day of _____, 19___,
and that such resolutions have not been rescinded or amended and are now in full force and effect:

WHEREAS, the Corporation has full corporate power and authority under its Charter, By-laws and the laws of its domicile to enter into contracts for the purchase, receipt, sale and delivery of commodity future contracts, commodities and related investments;

NOW THEREFORE, IT IS RESOLVED AS FOLLOWS:

RESOLVED, that it is in the best interest of this corporation to engage in trading, and otherwise dealing in, commodities, commodity futures contracts and related investments;

FURTHER RESOLVED, that, in order to induce CSA, Inc. to act as broker on behalf of the Corporation, the execution and delivery of a Client Information Sheet (Corporate Account), Risk Disclosure Statement, Client Agreement, Trading Authorization, Confirmation of

Trading Authority, Trading Advisor Letter and Authorization to Transfer Funds is hereby authorized and _____

_____ is hereby directed to execute such instruments by and on behalf of the

Corporation and to deliver the same to CSA, Inc., the Corporation hereby ratifying all action of _____
taken with regard to the account.

Secretary

(Corporate Seal)

Date

Exhibit 10–6

Form **W-9**	
(October 1983) Department of the Treasury Internal Revenue Service	**Payer's Request for Taxpayer Identification Number**

Please print or type

Name as shown on account (if joint account, also give joint owner's name) .

Address

City, State, and ZIP code

List account number(s) here (See Instructions) ▶ ....

PART I.—Taxpayer Identification Number

Enter the taxpayer identification number in the appropriate box. For most individual taxpayers, this is the social security number.

Note: *If the account is in more than one name, see the chart on page 2 for guidelines on which number to give the payer.*

Social security number
: :

OR

Employer identification number
:

PART II.—Backup Withholding On Accounts Opened After 12/31/83

Check the box if you are NOT subject to backup withholding under the provisions of section 3406(a)(1)(C) of the Internal Revenue Code . . . . ▶ ☐

(See **Highlight** below.)

Certification.—Under the penalties of perjury, I certify that the information provided on this form is true, correct, and complete.

Signature ▶   Date ▶

Instructions *(Section references are to the Internal Revenue Code.)*

Highlight for Interest or Dividend Accounts Opened After 12/31/83—Backup Withholding

You may be notified that you are subject to backup withholding under section 3406(a)(1)(C) because you have underreported interest or dividends or you were required to but failed to file a return which would have included a reportable interest or dividend payment. If you have NOT been so notified, check the box in PART II. **Note:** Backup withholding may apply to existing accounts as well as accounts opened after December 31, 1983.

Caution: There are other situations where you may be subject to backup withholding. Please read the instructions below carefully.

Purpose of Form

Use this form to report the taxpayer identification number (TIN) of the record owner of the account to the payer (or broker).

Beginning January 1, 1984, payers must generally withhold 20% of taxable interest, dividend, and certain other payments if you fail to furnish payers with the correct taxpayer identification number (this is referred to as backup withholding). For most individual taxpayers, the taxpayer identification number is the social security number.

To prevent backup withholding on these payments, be sure to notify payers of the correct taxpayer identification number and, for accounts you open after December 31, 1983, properly certify that you are not subject to backup withholding under section 3406(a)(1)(C).

You may use this form to certify that the taxpayer identification number you are giving the payer is correct and, for accounts opened after December 31, 1983, that you are not subject to backup withholding.

If the payer provides a different form than Form W-9 to request the taxpayer identification number, please use it.

Backup Withholding

You are subject to backup withholding if:

(1) You fail to furnish your taxpayer identification number to the payer, OR

(2) The Internal Revenue Service notifies the payer that you furnished an incorrect taxpayer identification number, OR

(3) You are notified that you are subject to backup withholding (under section 3406(a)(1)(C)), OR

(4) For an interest or dividend account opened after December 31, 1983, you fail to certify to the payer that you are **not** subject to backup withholding under (3) above, or fail to certify your taxpayer identification number.

For payments other than interest or dividends, you are subject to backup withholding only if (1) or (2) above applies.

(See the section on the back titled "Payees Exempt from Backup Withholding.")

Payments of Interest, Dividends, and Patronage Dividends

Accounts Opened Before January 1, 1984

To certify that the taxpayer identification number is correct for accounts opened before January 1, 1984, fill out your name and address, enter your account number(s) (if applicable), complete Part I, sign and date the form and return it to the payer.

Accounts Opened After December 31, 1983

To certify that the taxpayer identification number is correct and that you are not subject to backup withholding under section 3406(a)(1)(C) for accounts opened after December 31, 1983, fill out your name and address, enter your account number(s) (if applicable), complete Parts I and II, sign and date the form and return it to the payer.

If you are subject to backup withholding and are merely providing your correct taxpayer identification number to the payer, fill out your name, address, enter your account number(s) (if applicable), and complete Part I.

Other Payments

If you are merely providing your correct taxpayer identification number to the payer for payments other than interest, dividends, and patronage dividends, you need not sign this form. Fill out your name and address, enter your account number(s) (if applicable), complete Part I and return the form to the payer.

Account Numbers

If you have more than one account with the same payer (for example, a savings account and a certificate of deposit at the same bank), the payer may request a separate Form W-9 for each account depending on how the payer's records are kept.

What Number to Give the Payer

Give the payer the social security number or employer identification number of the record owner of the account. If the account belongs to you as an individual, give your social security number. If the account is in more than one name or is not in the name of the actual owner, see the chart on page 2 for guidelines on which number to report.

Obtaining a Number

If you don't have a taxpayer identification number or you don't know your number, obtain **Form SS-5,** Application for a Social Security Number Card, or **Form SS-4,** Application for Employer Identification Number, at the local office of the Social Security Administration or the Internal Revenue Service and apply for a number. Write "applied for" in Part I in place of your number. When you get a number, submit a new Form W-9 to the payer.

(Give this form to the payer, not to the Internal Revenue Service)   Form **W-9** (10-83)

Exhibit 10–6, *Concluded*

Penalties

(1) **Penalty for Failure to Furnish Taxpayer Identification Number.**—If you fail to furnish your taxpayer identification number to a payer, you are subject to a penalty of $50 for each such failure unless your failure is due to reasonable cause and not to willful neglect.

(2) **Failure to Report Certain Dividend and Interest Payments.**—If you fail to include any portion of an includible payment for interest, dividends, or patronage dividends in gross income, such failure will be treated as being due to negligence and will be subject to a penalty of 5% on any portion of an underpayment attributable to that failure unless there is clear and convincing evidence to the contrary.

(3) **Civil Penalty for False Information With Respect to Withholding.**—If you make a false statement with no reasonable basis which results in no imposition of backup withholding, you are subject to a penalty of $500.

(4) **Criminal Penalty for Falsifying Information.**—Falsifying certifications or affirmations may subject you to criminal penalties including fines and/or imprisonment.

Payees Exempt from Backup Withholding

Payees specifically exempted from backup withholding on **ALL** payments include the following:

● A corporation.
● A financial institution.
● An organization exempt from tax under section 501(a), or an individual retirement plan.
● The United States or any agency or instrumentality thereof.
● A State, the District of Columbia, a possession of the United States, or any subdivision or instrumentality thereof.
● A foreign government, a political subdivision of a foreign government, or any agency or instrumentality thereof.
● An international organization or any agency or instrumentality thereof.
● A registered dealer in securities or commodities registered in the U.S. or a possession of the U.S.
● A real estate investment trust.
● A common trust fund operated by a bank under section 584(a).
● An exempt charitable remainder trust, or a non-exempt trust described in section 4947(a)(1).
● An entity registered at all times under the Investment Company Act of 1940.
● A foreign central bank of issue.

Payments of **dividends and patronage dividends** not generally subject to backup withholding include the following:

● Payments to nonresident aliens subject to withholding under section 1441.
● Payments to partnerships not engaged in a trade or business in the U.S. and which have at least one nonresident partner.
● Payments of patronage dividends where the amount received is not paid in money.
● Payments made by certain foreign organizations.

Payments of **interest** not generally subject to backup withholding include the following:

● Payments of interest on obligations issued by individuals. Note: *You may be subject to backup withholding if this interest is $600 or more and is paid in the course of the payer's trade or business and you have not provided your correct taxpayer identification number to the payer.*
● Payments of tax-exempt interest (including exempt-interest dividends under section 852).
● Payments described in section 6049(b)(5) to nonresident aliens.
● Payments on tax-free covenant bonds under section 1451.
● Payments made by certain foreign organizations.

Exempt payees described above should file Form W-9 to **avoid** possible **erroneous** backup withholding. Because certain payments exempt from backup withholding are nevertheless subject to information reporting, if you file this form with the payer, furnish your taxpayer identification number, write "exempt" on the face of the form, and return it to the payer. If the payments are interest, dividends, or patronage dividends, also sign and date the form.

Certain payments other than interest, dividends, and patronage dividends that are not subject to information reporting are also not subject to backup withholding. For details, see the regulations under sections 6041, 6041A(a), 6045, and 6050A.

Privacy Act Notice.— Section 6109 requires most recipients of dividend, interest, or other payments to give taxpayer identification numbers to payers who must report the payments to IRS. IRS uses the numbers for identification purposes. Payers must be given the numbers whether or not recipients are required to file tax returns. Beginning January 1, 1984, payers must generally withhold 20% of taxable interest, dividend, and certain other payments to a payee who does not furnish a taxpayer identification number to a payer. Certain penalties may also apply.

Guidelines for Determining the Proper Identification Number to Give the Payer.— Social security numbers have nine digits separated by two hyphens: i.e., 000-00-0000. Employer identification numbers have nine digits separated by only one hyphen: i.e., 00-0000000. The table below will help you determine the number to give the payer.

For this type of account:	Give the SOCIAL SECURITY number of—
1. An individual's account	The individual
2. Two or more individuals (joint account)	The actual owner of the account or, if combined funds, any one of the individuals[1]
3. Husband and wife (joint account)	The actual owner of the account or, if joint funds, either person [1]
4. Custodian account of a minor (Uniform Gift to Minors Act)	The minor[2]
5. Adult and minor (joint account)	The adult or, if the minor is the only contributor, the minor[1]
6. Account in the name of guardian or committee for a designated ward, minor, or incompetent person	The ward, minor, or incompetent person[3]
7. a. The usual revocable savings trust account (grantor is also trustee)	The grantor-trustee[1]
b. So-called trust account that is not a legal or valid trust under State law	The actual owner[1]
8. Sole proprietorship account	The owner[4]

For this type of account:	Give the EMPLOYER IDENTIFICATION number of—
9. A valid trust, estate, or pension trust	Legal entity (Do not furnish the identifying number of the personal representative or trustee unless the legal entity itself is not designated in the account title.)[5]
10. Corporate account	The corporation
11. Religious, charitable, or educational organization account	The organization
12. Partnership account held in the name of the business	The partnership
13. Association, club, or other tax-exempt organization	The organization
14. A broker or registered nominee	The broker or nominee
15. Account with the Department of Agriculture in the name of a public entity (such as a State or local government, school district, or prison) that receives agricultural program payments	The public entity

[1] List first and circle the name of the person whose number you furnish.
[2] Circle the minor's name and furnish the minor's social security number.
[3] Circle the ward's, minor's, or incompetent person's name and furnish such person's social security number.
[4] Show the name of the owner.
[5] List first and circle the name of the legal trust, estate, or pension trust.

Note: If no name is circled when there is more than one name, the number will be considered to be that of the first name listed.

Exhibit 10–7
Part 190 Disclosure Statement

THIS STATEMENT IS FURNISHED TO YOU BECAUSE RULE 190.10 (c) OF THE COMMODITY FUTURES TRADING COMMISSION REQUIRES IT FOR REASONS OF FAIR NOTICE UNRELATED TO THIS COMPANY'S CURRENT FINANCIAL CONDITION.

1. YOU SHOULD KNOW THAT IN THE UNLIKELY EVENT OF THIS COMPANY'S BANKRUPTCY, PROPERTY, INCLUDING PROPER-TY SPECIFICALLY TRACEABLE TO YOU, WILL BE RETURNED, TRANSFERRED OR DISTRIBUTED TO YOU, OR ON YOUR BEHALF, ONLY TO THE EXTENT OF YOUR PRO RATA SHARE OF ALL PRO-PERTY AVAILABLE FOR DISTRIBUTION TO CUSTOMERS.

2. NOTICE CONCERNING THE TERMS FOR THE RETURN OF SPECIFICALLY IDENTIFIABLE PROPERTY WILL BE BY PUBLICATION IN A NEWSPAPER OF GENERAL CIRCULATION.

3. THE COMMISSION'S REGULATIONS CONCERNING BANKRUPTCIES OF COMMODITY BROKERS CAN BE FOUND AT 17 CODE OF FEDERAL REGULATIONS PART 190.

Gentlemen:

I have carefully examined the provisions of the document by which I have given trading authority or control over my account to

| Name | Address |

and understand fully the obligations which I have assumed by executing that document.

I understand that your firm is in no way responsible for any loss to me occasioned by the actions of the individual or organization named above and that your firm does not, by implication or otherwise, endorse the operating methods of such individual or organization. I further understand that neither the Chicago Board of Trade nor the Chicago Mercantile Exchange has juris-diction over a non-member who is not employed by one of its members and that if I give to such individual or organization authority to exercise any of my rights over my account, I do so at my own risk.

| Date | Signature of Customer |

Exhibit 10–8
Arbitration Agreement

Any controversy or claim arising out of or relating to the foregoing Agreement, or the breach thereof, shall be settled by arbitration pursuant to the rules of a qualified forum selected as hereinafter provided, and judgment upon the award rendered by the arbitrators may be entered in any court having jurisdiction thereof. Such arbitration shall be conducted in New York City, unless such rules shall otherwise require.

At such time as the Customer may notify Gerald Commodities, Inc. that he or she intends to submit a claim to arbitration, or at such time as Gerald Commodities,claim to arbitration, the Customer will have the opportunity to elect a qualified forum for conducting the proceeding in accordance with the provisions of Section 180.3(b)(4) of the Regulations of the Commodity Futures Trading Commisison. If the Customer fails so to elect a forum within the time prescribed under such provisions, Gerald Commodities, Inc. shall have the right to select the forum.

THREE FORUMS EXIST FOR THE RESOLUTION OF COMMODITY DISPUTES: CIVIL COURT LITIGATION, REPARATIONS AT THE COMMODITY FUTURES TRADING COMMISSION (CFTC) AND ARBITRATION CONDUCTED BY A SELF-REGULATORY OR OTHER PRIVATE ORGANIZATION.

THE CFTC RECOGNIZES THAT THE OPPORTUNITY TO SETTLE DISPUTES BY ARBITRATION MAY IN SOME CASES PROVIDE MANY BENEFITS TO CUSTOMERS INCLUDING THE ABILITY TO OBTAIN AN EXPEDITIOUS AND FINAL RESOLUTION OF DISPUTES WITHOUT INCURRING SUBSTANTIAL COSTS. THE CFTC REQUIRES, HOWEVER, THAT EACH CUSTOMER INDIVIDUALLY EXAMINE THE RELATIVE MERITS OF ARBITRATION AND THAT YOUR CONSENT TO THIS ARBITRATION AGREEMENT BE VOLUNTARY.

BY SIGNING THIS AGREEMENT, YOU: (1) MAY BE WAIVING YOUR RIGHT TO SUE IN A COURT OF LAW: AND (2) ARE AGREEING TO BE BOUND BY ARBITRATION OF ANY CLAIMS OR COUNTERCLAIMS WHICH YOU OR /GERALD COMMODITIES INC/ MAY SUBMIT TO ARBITRATION UNDER THIS AGREEMENT. YOU ARE NOT, HOWEVER, WAIVING YOUR RIGHT TO ELECT INSTEAD TO PETITION THE CFTC TO INSTITUTE REPARATIONS PROCEEDINGS UNDER SECTION 14 OF THE COMMODITY EXCHANGE ACT WITH RESPECT TO ANY DISPUTE WHICH MAY BE ARBITRATED PURSUANT TO THIS AGREEMENT. IN THE EVENT A DISPUTE ARISES, YOU WILL BE NOTIFIED IF GERALD COMMODITIES, INC. INTENDS TO SUBMIT THE DISPUTE TO ARBITRATION. IF YOU BELIEVE A VIOLATION OF THE COMMODITY EXCHANGE ACT IS INVOLVED AND IF YOU PREFER TO REQUEST A SECTION 14 "REPARATIONS" PROCEEDING BEFORE THE CFTC, YOU WILL HAVE 45 DAYS FROM THE DATE OF SUCH NOTICE IN WHICH TO MAKE THAT ELECTION.

YOU NEED NOT SIGN THIS AGREEMENT TO OPEN AN ACCOUNT WITH GERALD COMMODITIES, INC. SEE 17 CFR 180.1-180.5.

Customer: _____

Date: _____

Exhibit 10–9
Options Disclosure Statement

OPTIONS DISCLOSURE STATEMENT

BECAUSE OF THE VOLATILE NATURE OF THE COMMODITIES
MARKETS, THE PURCHASE AND GRANTING OF COMMODITY OPTIONS IN-
VOLVE A HIGH DEGREE OF RISK. COMMODITY OPTION TRANSACTIONS
ARE NOT SUITABLE FOR MANY MEMBERS OF THE PUBLIC. SUCH TRANS-
ACTIONS SHOULD BE ENTERED INTO ONLY BY PERSONS WHO HAVE READ
AND UNDERSTOOD THIS DISCLOSURE STATEMENT AND WHO UNDERSTAND
THE NATURE AND EXTENT OF THEIR RIGHTS AND OBLIGATIONS AND OF
THE RISKS INVOLVED IN THE OPTION TRANSACTIONS COVERED BY
THIS DISCLOSURE STATEMENT.

BOTH THE PURCHASER AND THE GRANTOR SHOULD KNOW
WHETHER THE PARTICULAR OPTION IN WHICH THEY CONTEMPLATE
TRADING IS AN OPTION WHICH, IF EXERCISED, RESULTS IN THE
ESTABLISHMENT OF A FUTURES CONTRACT (AN "OPTION ON A FU-
TURES CONTRACT") OR RESULTS IN THE MAKING OR TAKING OF
DELIVERY OF THE ACTUAL COMMODITY UNDERLYING THE OPTION
(AN "OPTION ON A PHYSICAL COMMODITY"). BOTH THE PURCHAS-
ER AND THE GRANTOR OF AN OPTION ON A PHYSICAL COMMODITY
SHOULD BE AWARE THAT, IN CERTAIN CASES, THE DELIVERY OF THE
ACTUAL COMMODITY UNDERLYING THE OPTION MAY NOT BE REQUIRED
AND THAT, IF THE OPTION IS EXERCISED, THE OBLIGATIONS OF
THE PURCHASER AND GRANTOR WILL BE SETTLED IN CASH.

A PERSON SHOULD NOT PURCHASE ANY COMMODITY OPTION
UNLESS HE IS ABLE TO SUSTAIN A TOTAL LOSS OF THE PREMIUM

Exhibit 10–9 *Continued*
Options Disclosure Statement

AND TRANSACTION COSTS OF PURCHASING THE OPTION. A PERSON
SHOULD NOT GRANT ANY COMMODITY OPTION UNLESS HE IS ABLE
TO MEET ADDITIONAL CALLS FOR MARGIN WHEN THE MARKET MOVES
AGAINST HIS POSITION AND, IN SUCH CIRCUMSTANCES, TO SUSTAIN
A VERY LARGE FINANCIAL LOSS.

A PERSON WHO PURCHASES AN OPTION SHOULD BE AWARE
THAT IN ORDER TO REALIZE ANY VALUE FROM THE OPTION, IT WILL
BE NECESSARY EITHER TO OFFSET THE OPTION POSITION OR TO EX-
ERCISE THE OPTION. IF AN OPTION PURCHASER DOES NOT UNDER-
STAND HOW TO OFFSET OR EXERCISE AN OPTION, THE PURCHASER
SHOULD REQUEST AN EXPLANATION FROM THE FUTURES COMMISSION
MERCHANT OR THE INTRODUCING BROKER. CUSTOMERS SHOULD BE
AWARE THAT IN A NUMBER OF CIRCUMSTANCES, SOME OF WHICH WILL
BE DESCRIBED IN THIS DISCLOSURE STATEMENT, IT MAY BE DIFFI-
CULT OR IMPOSSIBLE TO OFFSET AN EXISTING OPTION POSITION ON
AN EXCHANGE.

THE COMMODITY FUTURES TRADING COMMISSION REQUIRES
THAT ALL CUSTOMERS RECEIVE AND ACKNOWLEDGE RECEIPT OF A COPY
OF THIS DISCLOSURE STATEMENT BUT DOES NOT INTEND THIS STATE-
MENT AS A RECOMMENDATION OR ENDORSEMENT OF EXCHANGE-TRADED
COMMODITY OPTIONS.

Contents Of Disclosure Statement
1. Some of the risks of option trading.
2. Description of commodity options.

Exhibit 10–9 *Continued*
Options Disclosure Statement

3. The mechanics of option trading.

4. Margin requirements.

5. Profit potential of an option position.

6. Deep-out-of-the-money options.

7. Glossary of terms.

(1) <u>SOME OF THE RISKS OF OPTION TRADING</u>.

THE GRANTOR OF AN OPTION SHOULD BE AWARE THAT, IN MOST CASES, A COMMODITY OPTION MAY BE EXERCISED AT ANY TIME FROM THE TIME IT IS GRANTED UNTIL IT EXPIRES. THE PURCHASER OF AN OPTION SHOULD BE AWARE THAT SOME OPTION CONTRACTS MAY PROVIDE ONLY A LIMITED PERIOD OF TIME FOR EXERCISE OF THE OPTION.

THE PURCHASER OF A PUT OR A CALL IS SUBJECT TO THE RISK OF LOSING THE ENTIRE PURCHASE PRICE OF THE OPTION -- THAT IS THE PREMIUM PAID FOR THE OPTION PLUS ALL TRANS-ACTION COSTS.

Specific market movements of the underlying future or underlying physical commodity cannot be predicted accurately.

The grantor of a call option who does not have a long position in the underlying futures contract or underlying physical commodity is subject to risk of loss should the price of the underlying futures contract or underlying physical commodity increase by an amount greater than the

Exhibit 10-9 *Continued*
Options Disclosure Statement

premium received for granting the call option.

The grantor of a call option who has a long position in the underlying futures contract or underlying
physical commodity is subject to the full risk of a decline in price of the underlying position. In exchange
for the premium received for granting a call option, the
option grantor gives up all of the potential gain resulting from an increase in the price of the underlying futures contract or underlying physical commodity above
the option strike price if the option is exercised against
the grantor.

The grantor of a put option who does not have a
short position in the underlying futures contract or underlying physical commodity (e.g., commitment to sell the
physical) is subject to risk of loss should the price of
the underlying futures contract or underlying physical
commodity decrease by an amount in excess of the premium
received for granting the put option.

The grantor of a put option on a futures contract
who has a short position in the underlying futures contract
is subject to the full risk of a rise in the price of the
underlying position. In exchange for the premium received
for granting a put option on a futures contract the option
grantor gives up all of the potential gain resulting from

Exhibit 10–9 *Continued*
Options Disclosure Statement

a decrease in the price of the underlying futures contract
below the option strike price if the option is exercised
against the grantor. The grantor of a put option on a
physical commodity who has a short position (e.g., commitment to sell the physical) is subject to the full
risk of a rise in the price of the physical commodity
which must be obtained to fulfill the commitment. In
exchange for the premium, the grantor of a put option on
a physical commodity gives up all of the potential gain
which would have resulted from a decrease in the price
of the commodity below the option strike price if the
option is exercised against the grantor.

    (2)   DESCRIPTION OF COMMODITY OPTIONS.

Prior to entering into any transaction involv-
ing a commodity option, an individual should thoroughly
understand the nature and type of option and the underlying futures contract or underlying physical commodity
involved. The futures commission merchant or the introducing broker is required to provide, and the individual
contemplating an option transaction should obtain, a
description of the following:

        (i) The futures contract or the
physical commodity which is the subject of the
option;

        (ii) The quantity of the underlying
futures contract or underlying physical commodity which may be purchased or sold upon

Exhibit 10–9 *Continued*
Options Disclosure Statement

exercise of the option or, if applicable, whether exercise of the option will be settled in cash;

(iii) The procedure for exercise of the option contract, including the expiration date and latest time on that date for exercise. (The latest time on an expiration when an option may be exercised may vary; therefore, option market participants should ascertain from their futures commission merchant or their introducing broker the latest time the firm accepts exercise instructions with respect to a particular option.);

(iv) A description of the purchase price of the option including the premium, commissions, cost, fees and other charges. (Since commissions and other charges may vary widely among futures commission merchants and among introducing brokers, option customers may find it advisable to consult more than one firm when opening an option account.);

(v) A description of all costs in addition to the purchase price which may be incurred if the commodity option is exercised, including the amount of commissions (whether termed sales commissions or otherwise), storage, interest, and all similar fees and charges which may be incurred;

(vi) An explanation and understanding of the option grantor's initial margin requirement and obligation to provide additional margin in connection with such an option position, or a position in a futures contract, if applicable;

(vii) A clear explanation and understanding of any clauses in the option contract and of any items included in the option contract explicitly or by reference which might affect the customer's obligation under the contract. This would include any policy of the futures commission merchant or the introducing broker or rule of the exchange on which the option is traded that might affect the customer's ability to fulfill the option contract or to offset the option position in a closing purchase or closing sale transaction (for example, due to unforseen circumstances that require suspension or termination of trading); and

Exhibit 10–9 *Continued*
Options Disclosure Statement

(viii) If applicable, a description of the effect upon the value of the option position that could result from limit moves in the underlying futures contract.

(3) THE MECHANICS OF OPTION TRADING.

Before entering into any exchange-traded option transaction, an individual should obtain a description of how commodity options are traded.

Option customers should clearly understand that there is no guarantee that option positions may be offset by either a closing purchase or closing sale transaction on an exchange. In this circumstance, option grantors could be subject to the full risk of their positions until the option positions expire, and the purchaser of a profitable option might have to exercise the option to realize a profit.

For an option on a futures contract, an individual should clearly understand the relationship between exchange rules governing option transactions and exchange rules governing the underlying futures contract. For example an individual should understand what action, if any, the exchange will take in the option market if trading in the underlying futures market is restricted or the futures prices have made a "limit move."

Exhibit 10–9 *Continued*
Options Disclosure Statement

(4) MARGIN REQUIREMENTS.

Commodity Futures Trading Commission rules require the purchaser of an option to pay the full option
premium when the option position is open.

Before granting an option, an individual should
fully understand the applicable margin requirements, and
particularly should be aware of the obligation to put up
additional margin money in the case of adverse market
moves.

(5) PROFIT POTENTIAL OF AN OPTION POSITION.

An option customer should carefully calculate
the price which the underlying futures contract or underlying physical commodity would have to reach for the
option position to become profitable. This price would
include the amount by which the underlying futures
contract or underlying physical commodity would have
to rise above or fall below the strike price to cover
the sum of the premium and all other costs incurred
in entering into and exercising or closing (offsetting)
the commodity option position.

(6) DEEP-OUT-OF-THE-MONEY OPTIONS.

A person contemplating purchasing a deep-out-
of-the-money option (that is, an option with a strike
price significantly above, in the case of a call, or

Exhibit 10–9 *Continued*
Options Disclosure Statement

significantly below, in the case of a put, the current

price of the underlying futures contract or underlying

physical commodity) should be aware that the chance of

such an option becoming profitable is ordinarily remote.

On the other hand, a potential grantor of a

deep-out-of-the-money option should be aware that such

options normally provide small premiums while exposing

the grantor to all of the potential losses described in

section (1) of this disclosure statement.

(7) GLOSSARY OF TERMS

(i) Contract Market -- Any board of trade (ex-

change) located in the United States which has been des-

ignated by the Commodity Futures Trading Commission to

list a futures contract or commodity option for trading.

(ii) Exchange-Traded Options; Put Options;

Call Options -- The options discussed in this disclosure

statement are limited to those which may be traded on a

contract market. These options (subject to certain ex-

ceptions) give an option purchaser the right to buy in

the case of a call option, or to sell in the case of a

put option, a futures contract or the physical commodity

underlying the option at the stated strike price prior to

the expiration date of the option. Each exchange-traded

option is distinguished by the underlying futures con-

Exhibit 10–9 *Continued*
Options Disclosure Statement

tract or underlying physical commodity, strike price, expiration date, and whether the option is a put or a call.

(iii) Underlying Futures Contract -- The
futures contract which may be purchased or sold upon
the exercise of an option on a futures contract.

(iv) Underlying Physical Commodity -- The
commodity of a specific grade (quality) and quantity
which may be purchased or sold upon the exercise of an
option on a physical commodity.

(v) Class of Options -- A put or a call
covering the same underlying futures contract or underlying physical commodity.

(vi) Series of Options -- Options of the same
class having the same strike price and expiration date.

(vii) Exercise Price -- See strike price.

(viii) Expiration Date -- The last day when an
option may be exercised.

(ix) Premium -- The amount agreed upon between
the purchaser and seller for the purchase or sale of a
commodity option.

(x) Strike Price -- The price at which a
person may purchase or sell the underlying futures contract or underlying physical commodity upon exercise of

Exhibit 10–9 *Continued*
Options Disclosure Statement

a commodity option. This term has the same meaning as
the term "exercise price."

      (xi)   Short Option Position -- See Opening
Sales Transaction.

      (xii)   Long Option Position -- See Opening
Purchase Transaction.

      (xiii)   Types of Options Transactions --

      (A)   Opening Purchase Transaction --
A transaction in which an individual purchases an option and thereby obtains a long
option position.

      (B)   Opening Sale Transaction -- A
transaction in which an individual grants
an option and thereby obtains a short option
position.

      (C)   Closing Purchase Transaction --
A transaction in which an individual with
a short option position liquidates the position. This is accomplished by a closing
purchase transaction for an option of the
same series as the option previously granted.
Such a transaction may be referred to as an
offset transaction.

Exhibit 10–9 *Concluded*
Options Disclosure Statement

(D) <u>Closing Sale Transaction</u> --
A transaction in which an individual with
a long option position liquidates the position. This is accomplished by a closing sale
transaction for an option of the same series
as the option previously purchased. Such a
transaction may be referred to as an offset
transaction.

(xiv) <u>Purchase Price</u> -- The total actual cost
paid or to be paid, directly or indirectly, by a person
to acquire a commodity option. The price includes all
commissions and other fees, in addition to the option
premium.

(xv) <u>Grantor, Writer, Seller</u> -- An individual
who sells an option. Such a person is said to have a
short position.

(xvi) <u>Purchaser</u> -- An individual who buys an
option. Such a person is said to have a long position.

Chapter
11

Keeping Score: Knowing What Is Happening in Your Account

Becoming familiar with account reports.

Once all the necessary forms and statements have been completed, the account established, and the agreed-upon funds deposited, the advisor will be ready to conduct trades for an account. Of course, the investor will want to be kept informed of the status of the account—what trades are conducted, what fees and commissions are paid, where equity levels stand, and how the account performs overall.

For these purposes, the investor will receive a variety of statements and reports enabling him to keep close tabs on account activity and results. These reports will fall into four categories:

Confirmations of trades.

Profit and loss statements of realized trades.

Monthly statements.

Annual profit and loss statements for tax filing purposes.

Confirmation of Trades

The investor will receive a confirmation-of-trade statement each time a trade is executed in the account. The statement confirms a variety of items, including the exchange on which the trade was conducted; the date and time of the trade; the contract size, price, expiration date and terms, and the traded commodity, whether metals, currencies or any of the other futures markets. The trade confirmation also states whether the futures were bought or sold. (For examples, see Exhibits 11-1 through 11-3.)

Purchase & Sale Statements

Profit and loss statements are issued to the investor by the broker-manager whenever a round-turn or closed-out trade is made as a purchase & sale document. The investor will be informed of the type of realized trade conducted, in what market, and at what price, as well as the account's gains or losses resulting from the trade. In addition, commissions on such trades are indicated, and a cash-balance summary is furnished for the account. (For examples, see Exhibits 11-1 through 11-3.)

Frequently both of these statements are combined in what is called a "Combined Commodity Statement Confirmation and/or Purchase & Sale." The top portion of the statement reports the "Confirmation of Trades" and the lower portion the "Purchase & Sale."

Monthly Statements

Monthly statements provide a complete summary of account activity and status. Included are a monthly cash-balance report and a complete listing of all closed-out transactions, including commissions, the type and market value of open trades still held in the account, as well as a report of all securities in the account including any interest income. These monthly statements (along with an annual profit and loss statement) provide information required for tax purposes. (For example, see Exhibit 11–4.)

Annual Tax Information

A year-end statement should be provided by the brokerage firm, showing the same information being provided to the Internal Revenue Service in a 1099B form. The year-end statement includes:

Realized profit or loss for the year.

Unrealized profit or loss on open positions as of the last business day of the year (marked-to-market).

Aggregate profit or loss for the year. (For example, see Exhibit 11–5.)

As a convenience for clients, some brokerage firms summarize the T-bill interest earned and the fees paid to the trading advisor in a cover letter accompanying the annual year-end statement. (For example, see Exhibit 11–5A.)

For tax purposes all management fees are deductible from ordinary income whereas at the time of this writing commissions are deductible from capital gains on the account. The investor will, of course, want to consult an accountant or tax advisor, and should keep all statements—in particular the monthly account and annual profit and loss statements—on file for tax purposes.

Together, these daily and monthly statements provide a comprehensive and detailed accounting of all closed-out trading activity and results. Learning to read these reports will enable the investor to understand all aspects of the operations of the account. If the investor is confused or uncertain of any information contained in the statements, the broker, trading advisor, or account manager should be consulted, with the expectation of prompt, frank, and thorough explanations.

Daily Equity Run

Finally, the broker-manager produces a *daily equity run*, whether or not any trading activity has taken place in the account that day. The equity run provides the broker-manager with a complete report on the cash balance, open trade equity, total equity, and securities in the account. It is an excellent management tool. These detailed sheets provide the broker with a daily scorecard by which to monitor every aspect of the account. This report is kept by the broker and generally is not sent to the investor although it allows the broker-manager to immediately answer most questions the client may have about his account.

For examples of daily equity runs, we refer you to Chapter 7.

Exhibit 11–1

DATE		ACCOUNT NUMBER
JAN 29, 19XX		XYZ 1234

TAX ID 000-00-0000

COMBINED COMMODITY STATEMENT
CONFIRMATION AND/OR PURCHASE & SALE

DATE	GAINS IN 000'S		COMMODITY/OPTION DESCRIPTION	* P/C	* EX	TRADE PRICE	AMOUNT	
	BOUGHT	SOLD					DEBIT	CREDIT
01-25-XX	ACCOUNT BALANCE—SEGREGATED FUNDS							32486.59
+=+=+=+=+=+=+CONFIRMATION+=+=+=+=+=+=+=+=+=+=+=+CONFIRMATION=+=+=+=+=+=+=+=+=+=								
WE HAVE MADE THIS DAY THE FOLLOWING TRADES FOR YOUR ACCOUNT AND RISK								
	2 2*		JUL XX COPPER		G	63.30		
	1 1*		FEB XX HEAT OIL		L	72.95		
		1 1*	APR XX HEAT OIL		L	67.05		
+=+=+=+=PURCHASE & SALE+=+=+=+=+=+=PURCHASE & SALE+=+=+=+=+=+=+=+=+=+=+=+=+								
02-14-XX		1	JUL XX COPPER		G	60.35		
01-29-XX	1 1*	1*	JUL XX COPPER COMM. (70.00)		G	63.30 P & S	737.50	
10-19-XX		1	FEB XX HEAT OIL		L	76.50		
01-29-XX	1 1*	1*	FEB XX HEAT OIL COMM. (70.00)		L	72.95 P & S		1491.00
			FEES OR COMMISSIONS				140.00	
						NFA FEE	.56	
			NET PROFIT OR LOSS FROM TRADES					612.94 *
+=								
CURRENT ACCOUNT BALANCE—SEGREGATED FUNDS								33099.53

Exhibit 11–2

DATE		ACCOUNT NUMBER
DEC 11, 19XX		XYZ 1234

TAX ID 000-00-0000

COMBINED COMMODITY STATEMENT
CONFIRMATION AND/OR PURCHASE & SALE

DATE	GAINS IN 000'S		COMMODITY/OPTION DESCRIPTION	P/C •	EX •	TRADE PRICE	AMOUNT	
	BOUGHT	SOLD					DEBIT	CREDIT
12-07-XX	ACCOUNT BALANCE—SEGREGATED FUNDS							35988.28
+=+=+=+=+=+CONFIRMATION+=+=+=+=+=+=+=+=+=+=+CONFIRMATION=+=+=+=+=+=+=+=+=+=								
WE HAVE MADE THIS DAY THE FOLLOWING TRADES FOR YOUR ACCOUNT AND RISK								
	1 1 *		DEC XX J–YEN		E	40.480		
		1 1 *	MAR XX J–YEN		E	40.790		
	1 1 *		DEC XX GOLD–COMX		G	324.50		
		1 1 *	APR XX GOLD–COMX		G	332.90		
+=+=+=+=+=PURCHASE & SALE+=+=+=+=+=+=+=+=+=PURCHASE & SALE+=+=+=+=+=+=+=+								
09-07-XX		1	DEC XX J–YEN		E	41.440		
12-11-XX	1 1 *	1 *	DEC XX J–YEN COMM. (70.00)		E	40.480 P & S		1200.00
08-16-XX		1	DEC XX GOLD–COMX		G	364.50		
12-11-XX	1 1 *	1 *	DEC XX GOLD–COMX COMM. (70.00)		G	324.50 P & S		4000.00
			FEES OR COMMISSIONS				140.00	
						NFA FEE	.56	
			NET PROFIT OR LOSS FROM TRADES					5059.44 *
+=								
CURRENT ACCOUNT BALANCE—SEGREGATED FUNDS								41047.72

Exhibit 11–3

DATE		ACCOUNT NUMBER
JAN 8, 19XX		XYZ 1234

TAX ID 000-00-0000

COMBINED COMMODITY STATEMENT
CONFIRMATION AND/OR PURCHASE & SALE

DATE	GAINS IN 000'S		COMMODITY/OPTION DESCRIPTION	* P/C	* EX	TRADE PRICE	AMOUNT	
	BOUGHT	SOLD					DEBIT	CREDIT
12-27-XX	ACCOUNT BALANCE—SEGREGATED FUNDS							39363.38
+=+=+=+=+=+CONFIRMATION+=+=+=+=+=+=+=+=+=+=+=+=CONFIRMATION+=+=+=+=+=+=+=+=+=								
WE HAVE MADE THIS DAY THE FOLLOWING TRADES FOR YOUR ACCOUNT AND RISK								
		1	JAN XX LUMBER		H	162.10		
		1 *						
	1		MAY XX LUMBER		H	175.00		
	1 *							
+=+=+=+=PURCHASE & SALE+=+=+=+=+=+PURCHASE & SALE+=+=+=+=+=+=+=+=+=+=+=+=								
10-19-XX	1		JAN XX LUMBER		H	148.00		
01-08-XX		1	JAN XX LUMBER		H	162.10		
	1 *	1 *	COMM. (70.00)			P & S		1833.00
			FEES OR COMMISSIONS				70.00	
			NFA FEE				.28	
			NET PROFIT OR LOSS FROM TRADES					1762.72 *
+=								
CURRENT ACCOUNT BALANCE—SEGREGATED FUNDS								41126.10

Exhibit 11–4

PERIOD ENDING		ACCOUNT NUMBER
DEC 31, 19XX		XYZ 1234

TAX ID 000-00-0000

MONTHLY COMMODITY STATEMENT
ACTIVITY AND OPEN POSITIONS

SEGREGATED ACCOUNT

DATE	BOUGHT LONG	SOLD SHORT	COMMODITY/OPTION DESCRIPTION	P/C	EX	PRICE	DEBIT	CREDIT
11-30-XX	BALANCE FORWARD							37300.67
12-04-XX	1	1	MAR XX NEW COCOA		B	P&S	1670.28	
12-06-XX	MATURED T BILL					CASH		50000.00
12-06-XX	PURCH USTB DUE 1/17/XX INCLUDE FEE					CASH	49559.33	
12-07-XX	1	1	JUL XX COPPER		G	P&S	82.78	
12-11-XX	1	1	DEC XX J-YEN		E	P&S		1129.72
12-11-XX	1	1	DEC XX GOLD–COMX		G	P&S		3929.72
12-13-XX	ADJUSTMENT	MEMORANDUM			E	ADJ		70.00
12-14-XX	1	1	JUL XX COPPER		G	P&S	182.78	
12-17-XX	ADJUSTMENT	MEMORANDUM			G	ADJ		12.50
12-19-XX	MNGMENT FEE CK 11009					CASH	513.81	
12-26-XX	MNGMENT FEE DEC CK 11056					CASH	490.28	
12-27-XX	MGNT FEE CK 11065					CASH	579.97	
12-31-XX	ACCOUNT BALANCE—SEGREGATED FUNDS							39363.38*
NET FUTURES PROFIT OR LOSS (–) FOR MONTH							3,206.10	
* * * * * * *	* * * * * * *	* * * * * * *	* OPEN POSITIONS * * * * * * * * * *	* *	* * * *	OPEN POSITIONS* * *	* * * * *	
11-30-XX		5	MAR XX WHEAT		A	3.53 1/4		275.00
	*	5	* OPEN TRADE EQUITY			3.47 3/4		275.00
11-19-XX		5	MAR XX CORN		A	2.83 1/4		700.00
	*	5	* OPEN TRADE EQUITY		A	2.69 1/4		700.00
11-20-XX		5	MAR XX SOYBEANS		A	6.31 1/2		2312.50
	*	5	* OPEN TRADE EQUITY			5.85 1/4		2312.50
11-23-XX	1		JUNE XX T–BONDS		A	72	1656.25	
	1	*	* OPEN TRADE EQUITY			70 11/32	1656.25	

Exhibit 11–4 *Concluded*

DATE	BOUGHT	SOLD	COMMODITY/OPTION DESCRIPTION	*P/C	*EX	PRICE	AMOUNT	
	LONG	SHORT					DEBIT	CREDIT
12-04-XX		1	MAR XX NEW COCOA		B	21.12		600.00
	*1		* OPEN TRADE EQUITY			20.52		600.00
11-30-XX	1		MAR XX COFFEE C		C	136.80		2043.75
	1	*	* OPEN TRADE EQUITY			142.25		2043.75
11-16-XX		1	MAR XX COTTON		D	66.25		40.00
	*1		* OPEN TRADE EQUITY			66.17		40.00
11-05-XX		1	MAR XX B–POUND		E	126.85		2862.50
	*1		* OPEN TRADE EQUITY			115.40		2862.50
11-16-XX		1	MAR XX S–FRANCS		E	41.520		3412.50
	*1		* OPEN TRADE EQUITY			38.790		3412.50
12-11-XX		1	MAR XX J–YEN		E	40.790		1150.00
	*1		* OPEN TRADE EQUITY			39.870		1150.00
12-14-XX		1	JUL XX COPPER		G	60.35		475.00
	*1		* OPEN TRADE EQUITY			58.45		475.00
12-11-XX		1	APR XX GOLD–COMX		G	332.90		1910.00
	*1		* OPEN TRADE EQUITY			313.80		1910.00
11-09-XX	2		JUN XX HOGS		H	51.80		1665.00
	2	*	* OPEN TRADE EQUITY			54.57 1/2		1665.00
10-19-XX	1		JAN XX LUMBER		H	148.00		962.00
	1	*	* OPEN TRADE EQUITY			155.40		962.00
11-23-XX		1	MAR XX KC VAL LN		J	184.25		500.00
	*1		* OPEN TRADE EQUITY			183.25		500.00
10-19-XX		1	FEB XX HEAT OIL		L	76.50		1335.60
	*1		* OPEN TRADE EQUITY			73.32		1335.60
			TOTAL OPEN TRADE EQUITY					18587.60
			ACCOUNT VALUE AT MARKET					57950.98
MATURITY *****************			SECURITIES DEPOSITED AS MARGIN ***********************					VALUE
01-17-XX			U S TREASURY BILLS					49559.33
			ACCOUNT VALUE					107510.31

Exhibit 11–5

DATE		ACCOUNT NUMBER
DEC 31, 19XX		XYZ 1234

YEAR–END STATEMENT
19XX   TAX ID 000-00-000

TAXPAYER'S INFORMATION	REGULATED	NON–REGULATED
THE FOLLOWING INFORMATION IS BEING FURNISHED TO THE INTERNAL REVENUE SERVICE IN 1099B FORMAT. REGULATED FUTURES CONTRACTS - *REALIZED PROFIT OR LOSS (–) IN 19XX. *UNREALIZED PROFIT OR LOSS (–) ON OPEN CONTRACTS AS OF 12/31/XX. *AGGREGATE PROFIT OR LOSS (–) 19XX. NOTE: COMMODITY OPTION INFORMATION IS NOT BEING REPORTED *	14,419.18 7,788.35 22,207.53	

Exhibit 11–5A
T–Bill Interest and Fees Paid to Trading Advisor

Account Number	XYZ 1234	
T-Bill Interest Earned:		$2,690.27
Fees Paid to Trading Advisor:		$4,538.84

Chapter
12

Managing Your Trading Advisor

What criteria are used in the selection and monitoring of an account's trading advisor?
Professional assistance—the worry-free approach.
How a professional broker-manager can help you achieve success.

Relative newcomers to the world of commodity futures investing will want to develop an efficient and comfortable method of selecting and monitoring the managed account trading advisor. In some cases, an investor may wish to pursue this task personally or may wish to involve a professional broker-manager to provide the expertise and day-to-day scrutiny of the markets and the account.

Selecting and Monitoring Trading Advisors

Just as there should be a strict set of criteria for selecting trading advisors, so there should be for managing and monitoring the activity in the account once it has been established.

For both purposes—selecting and monitoring the trading advisor—we suggest a system that can be successfully employed by either the individual investor or the managed account broker-manager.

The Advisor Questionnaire

The foundation of this selection, evaluation, and monitoring system is the development of what we call a trading advisor questionnaire. This questionnaire is designed to extract from the trading advisor all the crucial points of information that an investor or broker-manager will need to effectively evaluate the advisor, and the advisor's system, strategies, and performance.

Let's look at the necessary information concerning the trading advisor and his approach to trading a managed commodity futures account. The following is a partial list of the points that should be covered in the advisor questionnaire:

The advisor's personal and business background.

The advisor's experience in the commodity futures markets.

The advisor's method of trading and trading strategies.

The advisor's cash-management approach.

The volatility ratio of the trading approach.

The margin percentage of the accounts.

The ratio of the commissions generated to the equity in the account.

The dollar amounts of winning and losing trades.

The ratio of profitable to unprofitable trades.

The employment of "stops" and how they are used (that is, at what point in upside or downside trends does the advisor tend to close out losing positions).

Total performance reported over an extended period of time.

The investor's evaluation of a particular trading advisor—whether the investor is in the process of selecting an advisor, or monitoring the advisor's current performance—

should be based on these objective criteria.

This evaluation should also include a personal visit to the advisor's offices during an actual trading day.

Professional Assistance—The Worry-Free Approach

The investor who lacks experience and expertise may wish to engage the services of a professional manager or advisory service in the selection and management of a trading advisor. There are several options available.

Some brokerage or investment firms offer selection services which are based on computerized evaluation models, incorporating an evaluation system based on the type of criteria suggested in the preceeding section. Such services tend to be of greater value during the selection process. Their lack of management experience and brokerage expertise, however, is a drawback with respect to both account monitoring and day-to-day management.

Established financial advisors or consultants also offer account evaluation and management services, and can be useful in both selecting the right advisor and in evaluating and monitoring his handling of the account once established. More often, however, such consultants will not be directly involved in the futures markets and consequently may lack the degree of market expertise considered essential by the investor.

A registered futures commission merchant, who is a clearing member of an established exchange having a quality in-house brokerage operation and a complete money management service is the preferred choice for most investors. Such broker-managers can establish a complete management package encompassing the evaluation, selection, monitoring brokerage, and reporting functions that would otherwise be spread out among a host of independent services. Such a broker-manager will be able to offer professional, specialized knowledge of the futures markets and the backgrounds of the trading advisors with whom it works. It will be able to provide competitively priced brokerage services as well as full-time monitoring and management of the account. It is responsible only to the investor as a client, and is not committed to any particular trading advisor.

Such a professional manager then becomes the investor's expert surrogate; the best among them maintain a constant open door policy toward the investor. They know exactly what is happening in the account at all times, and are available to the investor to answer all questions and discuss any concerns. The broker-manager also maintains regular contact with the account's trading advisor to ensure that decisions are being made on the basis of sound trading criteria. He or she will also be able to translate trading strategies into a language the investor can readily understand.

The savings in terms of the investor's time and capital—and peace of mind—can be substantial, and is available from a broker-manager for no additional management or brokerage fee. It is this type of management review approach, administered by a professional broker-manager, that we feel best serves the needs of most investors considering a managed futures account program.

Chapter
13

What to Expect from Your Broker

The broker is your representative.

With any type of managed futures account, an investor should expect the broker, through whom the trades are executed and processed, to provide a variety of critical services. This should hold true whether the account uses a management review approach, whether the account is managed by a professional broker-manager, or whether the broker is contracted independently through the account's trading advisor.

First, the investor should expect to receive competitive commission rates from the broker. As we have indicated previously, the investor may wish to "shop around" to ensure that commission rates are truly competitive. In terms of expected commission rates, the broker-manager may offer rates ranging from $60 to $80 per round-turn trade, compared to $120 per round-turn for other brokers in the managed account field. Timely and efficient execution of trades should also be expected, as should the prompt mailings of all trade confirmations, periodic profit and loss statements, monthly account statements, and annual profit and loss statements.

The investor should expect the brokerage firm to maintain effective administrative support capable of identifying and correcting any trade processing problems, and to keep such problems to a minimum. The brokerage firm should be responsible for the timely and efficient payment of advisors' fees from the account, and should maintain its own fiduciary responsibility on behalf of the account and the execution of Treasury bills or other securities held in the account.

Above and beyond these brokerage services, a broker-manager offering a management review approach to a futures account should be expected to provide in-depth account monitoring and advisor evaluation services to the investor. Such a broker-manager will give the investor an added degree of insurance by offering continuous performance evaluations. This type of complete client account representation should encompass everything from trading advisor selection and evaluation, to trade processing and reporting, as well as identification and verification of fees and commissions.

Your broker-manager, then, becomes a special advisor to you, representing you and not the trading advisor. In this way, your time commitments are reduced and your chances of enhancing your returns are vastly improved by the broker-manager's full-time attention and expertise.

Chapter
14

Protecting the Investor
If Problems Arise

What can I do if . . .
The five levels of protection and how they operate.
How effective are they?

Any investor who is considering a commitment of $50,000, $100,000, or more, to a managed futures account will want to know how he or she is protected in the event that problems arise concerning the management of the account. In the minds of some investors, images may persist of the unregulated and chaotic commodities markets of the ninteenth and early twentieth centuries. For the investor lacking experience in today's highly regulated and rapidly growing futures markets, it is comforting to know that in the event of a problem the investor is protected at five different levels. These are:

1. Personal relationship with broker-manager and/or trading advisor.

2. A responsible brokerage firm where account is cleared.

3. Stringent self-regulation by regulated Futures Exchanges.

4. Commodity Futures Trading Commission (CFTC).

5. National Futures Associations (NFA).

In addition, as we stated earlier, most trading advisors have cut-off points where trading in the account ceases and the remaining funds are returned to the client. These cut-off points usually occur when original equity drops by one-third to one-half.

The Trading Advisor and Broker-Manager

The first and most basic protection you have as a managed account investor will be your relationship with your trading advisor and broker-manager. In the operation and management of your account they have accepted certain important fiduciary responsibilities. Before you establish your account be sure to make yourself familiar with these legal responsibilities and, by all means, consult with your attorney. Once your account is established and trading has begun, maintain regular contact with the broker-manager or trading advisor and try to familiarize yourself with the futures markets and how they work. If you have any questions, feel free to ask. *After all, it is your money*!

Brokerage Firm

The brokerage firm where your account's trades are executed and cleared also has a responsibility to you as a public customer. The firm must comply with strict federal and exchange rules and the regulations governing the operation of the futures markets. These standards are set and painstakingly monitored by each of three additional regulatory bodies established specifically to ensure the protection of the public investor through orderly, regulated futures markets.

Many firms employ a compliance staff to ensure that the brokerage firm continuously meets all industry and government standards. Ask for corporate and financial references—*and check them yourself!*

Regulated Futures Exchange

All futures trading for your account is conducted at federally regulated futures exchanges. The various exchanges have been assigned the responsibility of ensuring orderly trading in specific commodities and other futures contracts. These exchanges include the Chicago Board of Trade, the Chicago Mercantile Exchange and International Monetary Market, the Kansas City Board of Trade, the New York Commodity Exchange (Comex), the New York Mercantile Exchange, the Mid-American Commodity Exchange, and the New York Coffee and Sugar Exchange.

These exchanges are as thoroughly regulated, both internally and externally, as any of the leading stock exchanges. The exchanges maintain legal and compliance departments responsible for identifying any potential problems and serving as internal "watchdogs" for the benefit of public customers.

The exchanges themselves can serve, therefore, as legal and investigative aides for the investor attempting to resolve a problem or dispute.

The Commodity Futures Trading Commission

Ultimately, the federal government regulates the operation of the entire futures industry through an independent agency—the Commodity Futures Trading Commission (CFTC)—established in 1975 as a result of Congressional amendments to the Commodity Exchange Act of 1936. The CFTC performs a role similar to the Securities and Exchange Commission (SEC). It maintains regulatory authority over the various futures exchanges by designating specific contract markets, approving or altering exchange rules and regulations, and by protecting the public through its emergency powers to "maintain or restore orderly trading in or liquidation of any futures contract."

In addition, the CFTC maintains regulatory authority over all professionals in the futures industry and markets. The agency registers all broker-dealers, account executives, floor brokers, commodity pool operators, and commodity trading advisors, establishing and maintaining strict suitability and fitness standards for registration. The agency also sets and monitors financial requirements for all broker-dealers or futures commission merchants (FCMs), and sets strict reporting and disclosure requirements for all industry participants. For added public customer protection, the CFTC requires the segregation of customer funds, the daily settlement of each account, and oversees the statutory anti-fraud provisions of the law.

The CFTC is also empowered to conduct investigatory activities and engage in disciplinary proceedings, including the right to:

Deny, condition, suspend or revoke its registration of industry participants.

Impose civil monetary penalties.

Issue cease and desist orders.

Bring injunctive proceedings in Federal district court.

The National Futures Association

Lastly, the futures industry itself maintains a strong commitment to self-regulation through the National Futures

Association, a self-regulatory agency with quasi-governmental authority. The NFA plays a role similar to the National Association of Security Dealers (NASD). Registration with and membership in NFA are mandatory for all futures market professionals. For public investors, the NFA offers a special arbitration service for the out-of-court settlement of disputes or claims.

How Effective Are the Regulatory Bodies?

This multi-faceted regulatory system has been so successful in the protection of public investors that a recent study conducted jointly by three federal agencies—the Federal Reserve Board, the Securities and Exchange Commission, and the Commodity Future Trading Commission—concluded in a 700 page report that the nation's commodity futures markets need no additional regulation now and are ready for decades of continued successful growth.

Chapter
15

In Conclusion:
A Successful Future in
Managed Futures Accounts

*The creation of wealth and the preservation of capital, now as
always, are the fundamental goals of all investors.*
Why new approaches are necessary.

Today's investor faces an array of risks as well as opportunities that distinguish the current era from other periods. The post-war Bretton Woods monetary system, which provided a relatively firm link between the value of our currencies and a fixed price for gold, underwent its first real strains during the 1958 U.S. recession. Subsequently, the inflationary economic growth of the 1960s began to tear that system apart, leading to the full scale demise of the Bretton Woods arrangements in August of 1971.

The OPEC oil embargo of the early 1970s signalled the end of an era of cheap energy—a fitting climax to the rampant inflation of the previous decade. But the inflationary economic growth of the 1960s gave way to an even more insidious economic demon: the stagflation of the 1970s. Economic growth came to a virtual standstill, unemployment mounted, interest rates soared, and yet inflation stubbornly remained.

During this entire period, investors witnessed an unprecedented level of volatility and uncertainty in the major, traditional equity markets. Many investors sought protection from the effects of inflation on their holdings by beginning to diversify out of equities and into tax shelter programs, real estate, and precious metals. Some were fortunate enough to obtain seasoned, professional investment advice, and many such investors were, at least temporarily, able to achieve some degree of success.

The search for appropriate, effective investment alternatives continues today. Changing tax policies and legislation have made some tax shelters less attractive today than they were in the past, and new tax policies are being considered now that could change the face of such programs for many years to come. Real estate values have seen severe up and down swings. At the time of this writing, interest rates are down considerably from the late 1970s, when money market funds offered exceptional returns. Still, real interest rates remain high, and with staggering federal budget deficits one must assume that they will remain high for some time.

The stock market, long the bastion of traditional investment strategies, continues to confound experts with its combination of uncertainty and volatility. Millions of individual investors have withdrawn from the market, compared to past periods, leaving the large institutional investors with a greater say in the performance of the market. As these institutions adjust their massive portfolios—frequently just to improve quarterly earnings forecast—the market has become even more volatile.

Government securities such as Treasury bonds and bills seem to offer a relatively safe haven for the investor seeking to preserve capital in these uncertain times, but the federal government cannot long continue to issue such monumental amounts of debt instruments without negatively affecting yields—not to mention the overall health and well-being of the economy and the financial system.

Interest rate volatility itself is at least partly to blame for the ill state of the banking system, as witnessed during the virtual insolvency of huge institutions such as the Continental Illinois National Bank and various savings and loan institutions.

Today's investor, indeed, faces a disturbing array of risks and uncertainties. In order to preserve capital and create additional wealth, today's investor must look to new investment alternatives. Certainly, the growth and maturation of the commodity futures markets indicate that futures are an increasingly accepted and effective investment alternative.

But success in the futures markets is by no means guaranteed. The non-professional, individual investor seeking to profit in the commodity futures markets has been overwhelmingly unsuccessful. The vast majority of investors who attempt to navigate the complex world of commodity futures trading, without the advice and direction of experienced, professional managers inevitably turn up in the loss column.

Professionally managed commodity futures accounts are relatively new investment vehicles. They are not to be considered in the realm of highly speculative ventures. It is the opinion of the authors that properly managed accounts constitute relatively conservative instruments for achieving an investor's goal of capital preservation and wealth creation. When pursued in the context of a sound, overall investment plan, managed futures accounts can help to dramatically improve the risk/reward characteristics of your total portfolio holdings.

The commodity futures markets offer a unique set of opportunities for both profit and risk management, and the investor who is willing to seize these opportunities through the managed futures account may well end up ahead of the game—and indeed ahead of the rest of the pack.

It is for these investors that this book has been written.

Appendix

Some additional facts and fictions about futures.

Readers may have a variety of additional questions concerning managed futures accounts. The authors certainly encourage inquiries from interested readers. Here, however, we attempt to answer some of the more frequently asked questions.

Q: Will I actually ever have to take delivery of any commodities?

A: No, you will never get commodities dumped in your front yard if your account is managed according to the criteria we have set forth. Under our managed account approach, our trading advisors do not trade commodities in the months that they are due for delivery. Less than 3 percent of all futures contracts are delivered, and then only to approved warehouse facilities—none of which include your pool or front yard.

Q: What are "limits" and how do they protect investors?

A: Unlike the stock market where prices are permitted to rise and fall unrestrainedly, futures exchanges place daily limits on commodity prices to keep price fluctuations—up and down—within a controlled range.

These limits are designed to protect investors by preventing the amount of financial leverage inherent in futures trading from becoming disproportionately high.

Q: **What are "limit days" and do they represent any additional risks?**

A: Limit days occur when there is a temporary imbalance between buyers and sellers in the market—when supply exceeds demand or demand exceeds supply. This causes prices to rise or fall to their daily limits.

The principal risks to which investors are exposed on limit days are illiquidity and the possibility of holding losing positions.

Because of the diversified nature of managed futures accounts, the effect of limit days on the account would be minimal. Moreover, the trading advisors used by the authors have, 80 percent of the time, successfully anticipated limit days or have not been involved in limit days at all.

Q: **What are the main differences between commodities margins and securities margins?**

A: In the securities markets, margins are now 50 percent and represent an ownership position in a security acquired with a loan provided by the broker. Interest is charged on securities margins at a certain percent above the broker call loan rate.

In futures, on the other hand, the margin is a good

faith deposit, similar to a performance bond in real estate. For this reason, no interest is charged. The margin percentages for most commodities vary between 5 and 15 percent of the value of the contract. The exchanges set their own minimum margin requirements. These low margin requirements for commodities mean greater financial leverage for the investor, and provide greater amounts of assets to be acquired per dollar invested than in other investments.

Q: **Will I get "margin calls" from my broker asking me to put up more margin money?**

A: If you follow the approach to managed accounts presented in these pages, the answer is simply "No!" This program is designed and managed so that sufficient capital is always held in reserve, usually in the form of U.S. Government securities, such as short-term Treasury bills, or cash. The result: You will never get a "margin call" and will never have to invest additional funds unless you wish to. To our knowledge, and that of the trading advisors we are familiar with, no investor has had a "margin call" for a professionally managed account traded according to the methods outlined in this book.

Q: **What commodity futures are likely to be traded in my managed account?**

A: Futures contracts in some or all of these commodities groups are likely to be traded for your account:

> **Stock Indexes:** S&P 500, NYSE Composite, Kansas City Value Line, Major Market Index.

> **Interest Rates:** Treasury bills, Treasury bonds, GNMAs, Eurodollars.

Precious Metals: Gold, Silver, Platinum.

Currencies: Swiss franc, Deutsche mark, British pound, Japanese yen, Canadian dollar.

Grains and Oils: Wheat, Soybeans, Corn, Soybean Oil and Meal.

Meats: Pork Bellies, Live Cattle, Feeder Cattle, Hogs.

Foods: Coffee, Sugar, Cocoa.

Industrials: Cotton, Copper, Heating Oil, Light Crude, Lumber.

Options on a variety of Futures Contracts.

Index

⊡ Probus Publishing Company Presents

(continued on the following page)

Titles in Business

Revitalizing Your Business: Five Steps to Successfully Turning Around Your Company, by Edmund P. Freiermuth. ISBN 0-917253-05-1.

Compensating Yourself: Personal Income, Benefits and Tax Strategies for Business Owners, by Gerald I. Kalish. ISBN 0-917253-07-8.

Getting Your Banker to "Yes": Tactics for the Entrepreneur, by Adam E. Robins. ISBN 0-917253-11-6.

Using Consultants: A Consumer's Guide for Managers, by Thomas A. Easton and Ralph Conant. ISBN 0-917253-03-5.

Cutting Loose, by Thomas A. Easton and Ralph W. Conant. ISBN 0-917253-14-0.

What's What in America Business: Facts and Figures on the Biggest and the Best, by George Kurian. ISBN 0-917253-17-5.

Competing for Clients: The Complete Guide to Marketing and Promoting Professional Services, by Bruce Marcus. ISBN 0-917253-26-4.

For further information, call Probus Publishing Company at (312) 346-7985.